Helping Delinquents Change

A Treatment Manual of
Social Learning Approaches

THE CHILD & YOUTH SERVICES SERIES:

EDITOR-IN-CHIEF

JEROME BEKER, *Director and Professor, Center for Youth Development and Research, University of Minnesota*

- *Institutional Abuse of Children & Youth*, edited by Ranae Hanson
- *Youth Participation & Experiential Education*, edited by Daniel Conrad and Diane Hedin
- *Legal Reforms Affecting Child & Youth Services*, edited by Gary B. Melton
- *Social Skills Training for Children and Youth*, edited by Craig W. LeCroy
- *Adolescent Substance Abuse: A Guide to Prevention and Treatment*, edited by Richard Isralowitz and Mark Singer
- *Young Girls: A Portrait of Adolescence*, by Gisela Konopka
- *Adolescents, Literature, and Work with Youth*, co-edited by J. Pamela Weiner and Ruth M. Stein
- *Residential Group Care in Community Context: Implications From the Israeli Experience*, edited by Zvi Eisikovits and Jerome Beker
- *Helping Delinquents Change: A Treatment Manual of Social Learning Approaches*, edited by Jerome Stumphauzer
- *Qualitative Research and Evaluation in Group Care*, edited by Rivka Eisikovits and Yitzhak Kashti
- *The Black Adolescent Parent*, edited by Stanley F. Battle

Helping Delinquents Change
A Treatment Manual of Social Learning Approaches

Jerome S. Stumphauzer, PhD

The Haworth Press
New York • London

Helping Delinquents Change: A Treatment Manual of Social Learning Approaches has also been published as *Child & Youth Services,* Volume 8, Numbers 1/2, Fall 1985.

The Haworth Press, Inc., 12 West 32 Street, New York, NY 10001
EUROSPAN/Haworth, 3 Henrietta Street, London, WC2E 8LU England

Library of Congress Cataloging in Publication Data

Stumphauzer, Jerome S.
 Helping delinquents change.

 "Published also as v. 8, no. 1/2 of the Child & youth services."
 Bibliography: p.
 Includes index.
 1. Rehabilitation of juvenile delinquents.
2. Behavior modification. 3. Juvenile delinquency—Prevention. 4. Juvenile
corrections. I. Title.
HV9069.S793 1986   364.3'6   86-9939
ISBN 0-86656-405-5
ISBN 0-86656-473-X (pbk.)

Dedication

In honor of my mother, Emma,
and in memory of my father, John

About the Author

The focus of the author's career has been the behavioral treatment of delinquency. His published work has ranged from clinical behavior therapy to community-based programs for violent youth gangs, adolescent substance abuse, and training in behavior therapy. A graduate of Florida State University, he is Clinical Professor of Psychiatry and the Behavioral Sciences at the University of Southern California School of Medicine. His previous books include *Behavior Modification Principles: An Introduction and Training Manual* (English, 1977; Spanish, 1983), *Behavior Therapy With Delinquents* (1973), and *Progress in Behavior Therapy With Delinquents* (1979).

Helping Delinquents Change: A Treatment Manual of Social Learning Approaches

Child & Youth Services
Volume 8, Numbers 1/2

CONTENTS

Preface

Delinquent behavior is a major problem facing modern society and most believe it is very difficult to change. If you did not believe this, you would not be reading this book. It is also a most confusing area to understand—not only for parents and teachers, but also for counselors and professional therapists. There is a full array of conflicting theories and approaches to the problem. It was the goal in writing this book to remove the mystery in understanding delinquency, and then to provide direct, useful ways to help delinquents change. The concept of this book was stimulated by the on-line people who work directly with delinquents who repeatedly asked the author over the last several years to ''write a book for us.''

This book and the general social learning approach represent a marked shift from traditional orientations to the problem of delinquency which have stressed punishment (juvenile justice) or mental illness (medical model). The view promoted in this book is primarily positive and humanistic with its stress on learning of adaptive, prosocial behavior. Furthermore, the youths themselves are often engaged directly in selecting goals, methods, and in changing their own behavior. The title—*Helping Delinquents Change*—was chosen to reflect this orientation. The reader will also find a new stress on *non*delinquents who have managed to survive and even succeed in high-crime communities. The author believes there is much to learn from them—skills that could help delinquents change and, if learned by children, could prevent delinquency on a broader scale.

An attempt was made to produce an easy-to-read, nontechnical, utilitarian guide for practitioners. This is *not* a highly academic textbook or detailed research review. Technical jargon has been kept to a minimum, and no prerequisite background should be necessary. It is a practical introduction, sourcebook, and treatment manual. The directly pertinent literature is cited by way of example and reference is made to more extensive coverage of techniques, research, and review.

The intended audiences are the entry level clinicians/practitioners who work directly with delinquents: counselors, teachers, thera-pists, probation officers, those working in juvenile corrections, and students of delinquent behavior in psychology, sociology, criminol-ogy, and education. The book may lend itself particularly well as a training manual or as a supplementary text for courses related to juvenile delinquency. The book should also be useful to those familiar with a few of these approaches, but who now find that they must shift to other areas covered here.

There are four introductory chapters followed by nine chapters of particular techniques applicable in different settings—or in combi-nation. Each chapter has a summary which ends with a transition to the next topic and three readings for further review or "how-to-do-it" details. Numerous forms and outlines have been included throughout the book so that practictioners can utilize and evaluate them in their own work. A full list of references and an index are found at the back of the book.

Chapter One presents a basic introduction to understanding delinquent behavior and to the general social learning approach. This continues in Chapter Two with a similar approach to nondelinquent behavior. After all, this is the ultimate goal, isn't it—increasing good, productive, noncriminal behavior?

In Chapter Three we will get down to the specifics of evaluation and measuring the behavior of delinquents in a way that will both point the way to particular intervention strategies (tell us what to do next) and that will give us feedback on exactly what is improving behavior and what is not. This evaluation culminates in a behavioral assessment report.

Chapter Four will review the basic principles paramount to social learning theory—specifically as they apply to learning delinquent behavior and, central to this book, how they apply to changing or unlearning delinquent behavior.

Chapters Five through Thirteen will present the detailed "how-to-do-it" of nine social learning approaches to helping delinquents change: from the institution to the neighborhood. The final chapter, Chapter Thirteen, will also take a broader look at social learning approaches to community change and prevention—an area where we need to seek an ultimate answer to the delinquency "problem." Each of these chapters has three sections: they begin with an introduction to the topic, continue with examples of how others have applied the methods, and then conclude with specific tech-niques the reader might apply directly. The work of many practitioners is modeled as are case examples from the author's research and clinical practice.

On a personal note, let me say that I have waited a long time to write this book. Helping delinquents change has been a major part of my clinical and academic work (treatment, research, teaching, supervision, and writing) for the past fifteen years. I felt that it was not until now that the comprehensive set of social learning approaches to delinquent behavior presented here were developed and refined to a degree that they could be presented in one, relatively brief sourcebook for those working directly with delinquents. It will become obvious that my work has been greatly influenced by innovative colleagues in many parts of the world. I hope that they will also act as models for you.

The author has edited two volumes that may well serve as reference books for the reader because the works of experts in the area are fully reproduced: *Behavior Therapy With Delinquents* (1973) and *Progress In Behavior Therapy With Delinquents* (1979). The author has prepared a one hour audio cassette as well: *Six Techniques Of Modifying Delinquent Behavior* (1974). Also related to this work is the author's basic introduction to behavior modification that has been used to train probation officers, students, paraprofessionals, and mental health personnel: *Behavior Modification Principles: An Introduction And Training Manual* (1977).

Finally, it is often said that "delinquents are the most difficult people to change." The real aim of this book is to show you that this need not be true.

Jerome S. Stumphauzer
Los Angeles, 1986

Acknowledgements

When a book develops over several years it is difficult to pinpoint individuals who helped stimulate and keep it going. Teachers, models, colleagues, and students who were directly or indirectly responsible for this book are Wallace Kennedy, Albert Bandura, Michael Mahoney, Carl Thoresen, Cyril Franks, Robert Polakow, Ruth Sinay, Victor Sanchez, Maxine Brown, Esteban Veloz, Tom Aiken, Caesar Nunez, Richard Nunez, Philip Perez, Jr., Susan Spence, Isaac Seligson, Gail Garrison, Menette Bragg, Albert Duran, and a "cast of thousands" of not-so-delinquent delinquents over the past fifteen years. Thanks must also be given to Tran Cuc Tran who helped turn drafts and revisions into manuscript.

Helping Delinquents Change

A Treatment Manual of
Social Learning Approaches

CHAPTER 1

Understanding Delinquency:
A Behavioral Analysis

1. THE DELINQUENCY PROBLEM

"Juvenile delinquency" did not exist until 1899. That is when the special juvenile courts began in America and, prior to this date, young criminals were for the most part treated like adults. With the new courts came the new name for crime committed by young people. Juvenile courts were hailed as a great social reform in which the welfare of the child (not yet fully responsible for his or her behavior) became as much a concern as the law breaking itself. The court, in many cases, became the parent. Since that time, "juvenile delinquency" has remained a major concern to the public—ranking just under peace and national survival (Tunley, 1964).

The figures in the F.B.I.'s annual *Uniform Crime Report,* a gathering of police statistics, are often noted as suggestive of the extent of the problem. In 1984, for example, there were more than two million arrests of persons under 18 years of age. This, of course, is only the figure on *detected* and *reported* juvenile crime— and merely an estimate. Even more alarming, most believe, are reports throughout the world of increases in especially serious and violent crimes by young people: murder, rape, and armed robbery (Stumphauzer, 1981b).

A juvenile delinquent is a youth who does delinquent behavior. To be legally delinquent, the adolescent or child must have violated a statute of some governmental jurisdiction. These offenses can range from truancy and curfew violations to major crimes. It is the central thesis of this book that delinquency can be best understood as behavior occurring in a set of environmental circumstances that can be determined and changed in such a way as to decrease or

1

eliminate the delinquent behavior while, at the same time, increasing nondelinquent behavior.

2. THEORIES OF CRIME AND DELINQUENCY

Everyone, it seems, likes to theorize about the causes, development, and even the "roots" of crime and delinquency. It would appear that there are as many theories as there are schools of thought. What is needed most today is a theory for the understanding of crime and delinquency that would have everyday utility in changing or preventing criminal behavior. For purposes of discussion here, we can group theories of crime and delinquency into (a) biological theories, (b) social theories, and (c) psychological theories.

Biological theories suggest that criminal misconduct is somehow the result of flaws in the biology or chemistry of delinquents. At different times these flaws have been sought in heredity, brain damage, endocrine failure, body type, race, and even dietary imbalance. In general, little evidence has been found to support these views (Gibbons, 1970). This is not to say that biology plays no role in behavior or that, in some individual cases, one or more of these aspects could not play a causative role. For example, the quite rare XYY chromosomal condition has been *correlated* with crime but causation (that the XYY configuration *causes* criminal behavior) has not been demonstrated.

Social theories link criminal behavior to social structure, social alienation and to specific social problems such as poverty, unemployment, lower class status, racial/ethnic discrimination, and unemployment. While it is difficult to argue with these theories because they make so much "common sense," they are difficult to prove as well. Also, they fail to account for poor, unemployed, fatherless, minority youths in high crime communities who remain nondelinquent (Aiken, Stumphauzer, & Veloz, 1977).

Psychological theories likewise vary widely. The "mental illness" view, linked through psychiatry to medicine and biological theories, suggests that delinquents have some "underlying" mental disease which causes delinquent behavior. Indeed, the very term "delinquency" is used by many as if it were a disease entity and that it (the disease) caused crime. The psychoanalytic or Freudian view in particular suggests that delinquent behaviors are simply *symptoms* of underlying, unconscious psychopathology. One such popular view is that of the "superego lacunae" or the Swiss cheese theory of a pathological conscience with holes in it (Johnson & Szurek, 1952). Such hypothetical armchair constructs—taken quite seriously by psychoanalytic therapists—have added little to any useful understanding of delinquency. Besides, a "patching" of these imaginary holes would only lead to a build up of "psychic forces" and a subsequent "leak" in the form of yet another "symptom."

A second psychological theory centers on the antisocial personality: the psychopath or sociopath as they are sometimes called. This view holds that certain individuals repeatedly commit crimes because they cannot delay gratification, experience little anxiety, and suffer little or no guilt for their wrongdoing. Theories have linked psychopathic personalities to emotional deprivation/rejection by parents (McCord & McCord, 1964) and to a too slow rate of classical conditioning (Eysenck, 1964). More recently, Yochelson and Samenow (1976) have made an extensive case for a psychological theory of "the criminal personality."

Finally, psychological *learning* theories of crime have taken the view that criminal behavior, like most other behaviors, is learned following established psychological principles. Three major learning theories of crime are (a) the reinforcement or operant conditioning view (that criminal behavior is reinforced and gradually shaped (Skinner, 1953; Stumphauzer, 1977), (b) the view that crime is due to faulty classical conditioning of the "conscience reflex" and related to the extroversion/introversion dimension of personality (Eysenck, 1964), and (c) the social learning view that crime is learned in given *social* contexts through modeling, observation, and then reinforcement (Bandura, 1977; Nietzel, 1979). This chapter will, for the most part, present a social learning approach to the understanding of delinquent behavior as the most useful available today.

3. JUVENILE MISCONDUCT OR JUVENILE DELINQUENCY?

Many believe that today's youth can be divided basically into two groups: juvenile delinquents and "good kids." Actually, of course, it is not so simple. First of all, virtually all adolescents, at one time or another, do things that could be called "delinquent." They might shoplift a few times, vandalize property, get drunk, be truant from school, etc. Research, conducted anonymously with college students, indicates that nearly everyone breaks laws as a youth. Perhaps the difference between delinquency and misconduct is one of degree, frequency, age, and social circumstance. If the crimes were frequent, severe and in particular situations where they will be reported officially; then the youth doing them may finally be labeled delinquent. In addition, if the police arrest and eventually the courts convict the youth, they will be defined as delinquents.

For our purposes here we will view juvenile delinquency as *delinquent behavior* occurring on a continuum from occasional adolescent misconduct to severe, recurrent crime. It is perhaps a part of normal adolescent development (certainly universal) to try new behaviors, to do some wrong—even unlawful—things; to "test limits" of parents, schools, and their community. Most respond to those "limits," those natural punishments, and those social rewards (if there are any) for doing noncriminal, constructive behavior. A relatively small percentage continue to commit crimes, and those behaviors are eventually called delinquent. Too often the youth (and not his or her behavior) is called delinquent, and this label may actually make things worse: iatrogenic labeling. Keep in mind, also, that some behaviors are criminal for only children and adolescents and not for adults ("status crimes" such as truancy, incorrigibility, buying alcohol, curfew violations). Are delinquent behaviors best defined and handled by police and the courts?

4. WHY ARREST AND JUVENILE JUSTICE DON'T WORK

Because police, courts, and correctional facilities are such a common part of our society (they seemingly have always been there), most people believe (a) they are adequate as is, (b) we need more of them, more "law and order," or (c) they still "make sense" and should simply be improved.

First of all, we cannot assume that police are going to catch everyone or arrest a youth every time he commits even serious crimes. Also, it is quite clear that of those who are apprehended for the same criminal behavior, some will be arrested, some will be let go, and some cases will be handled "unofficially." Females, young children, middle and upper class youths, and nonminority members are more likely to be let free (Gibbons, 1970). Second, arrest may *not* act as a deterrent for some youths, especially if, as is often the case, they are soon released. In fact, this series of events (arrest, detention, release) may act as a reward by increasing status with peers (Stumphauzer, Aiken, & Veloz, 1977).

Once youths are arrested there is a good chance that the court will not convict them. Increased legal rights of youths on the one hand, and increased restrictions on police and prosecutors on the other hand, make conviction even less likely today.

During this costly legal ordeal—often taking months—the youth may be confined in a detention center or juvenile hall. If found "guilty" there is a high probability that the judge will return the youth to his or her *same* social setting and place him or her on probation. In more severe or repetitive cases, juvenile correction facilities (actually youth prisons) will be recommended. The National Council on Crime and Delinquency used to run a remarkable advertisement, a picture of a youth with a gun and a caption at the bottom stating: "Prison isn't a waste of time. A lot of kids come out learning a trade." A worse social learning program could not be designed: remove the youth from the very society to which he must learn to adapt, expose him to hundreds of criminal peer models and to criminal behaviors he hasn't learned (yet), and use punishment as the only learning principle to change behavior! Indeed, some research shows that staff in such institutions are even inconsistent at this, while peer inmates are quite consistent in their "anti-social shaping" program (Buehler, Patterson, & Furniss, 1966).

5. THE PROBLEMS WITH PROBATION

Probation has been heralded as the greatest contribution from American corrections to the world. Indeed, assigning "first offenders" and less serious cases to an officer who will supervise the youth's correctional program while he or she remains in the community seems to make "good social learning sense." Today, however, there are four major problems that prevent probation officers from effectively changing delinquent behavior. First, the probation "contract" (the "if you do this, then this will happen") is vague and not clearly spelled out. Too often it is "you better stay out of trouble (alternatively, keep your nose clean) or else." Second, punishment, or threat of punishment, is the *only* social learning principle utilized—and, as you will see, is the *least* effective principle. Third, probation officers are not trained specifically on how to change behavior, although this can be accomplished in a relatively brief period (Burkhart, Behles & Stumphauzer, 1976). Fourth, and especially with today's budget cuts, probation officers carry an incapacitatingly large caseload (as many as 400 clients!). To make things worse, much of probation officers' time is taken up with paper work having little direct utility. What, then, is the social learning approach to changing delinquent behavior?

6. THE SOCIAL LEARNING APPROACH

Briefly, the social learning approach can be stated: *delinquent behavior is acquired through psychological learning principles in a social context, and changing delinquent behavior requires application and variation of the same principles—also in a social context.* The task is (a) to determine how delinquent behavior was (and currently still is being) learned, (b) to select and utilize a reliable measure of the delinquent behavior, and (c) to apply the particular social learning techniques for helping delinquents change which are determined by the analysis of the behavior and current life circumstances (legal status, availability of various interventions, and present social environment at home, school, etc.).

7. THE ABC'S OF DELINQUENT BEHAVIOR

Before describing the actual social learning approaches to helping delinquents change, it will help to learn the ABC's of delinquent behavior. Stealing, a most common delinquent behavior, will be used as an example (see Figure 1).

"A" refers to antecedents or to what happens *before*. What precisely stimulates or triggers this particular delinquent behavior in this certain person at this particular moment? Antecedent events can be of many different kinds (or a combination) and are listed in Figure 1: social, emotional, situational, cognitive, and physiological. They act together in a complex but understandable way to stimulate or set off the delinquent behavior: in this case, stealing this car at this moment. "B" is the behavior which itself is

THE ABC's OF DELINQUENT BEHAVIOR

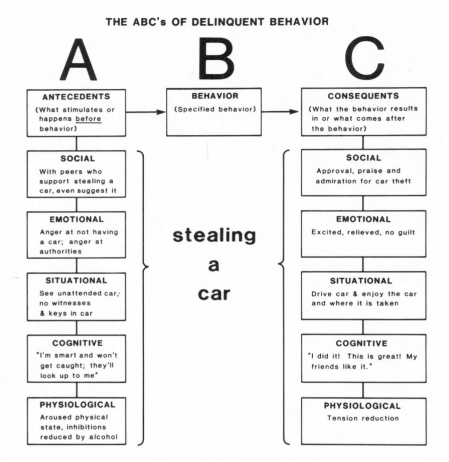

FIGURE 1. The ABC's of delinquent behavior.

often a complex chain of behaviors which go to make up "stealing a car."

"C" stands for consequents or for what happens after, what the behavior results in: the "payoff." However, the consequents are nothing as general as this term implies, but rather are specific, understandable events: again—social, emotional, situational, cognitive, and physiological. This, then, is how we come to *understand delinquency*. It removes the mystery attached to delinquent behaviors by other theories and answers, quite directly, questions like "How could this happen?" and "What can be done about it?" and

"Could it have been prevented?" This *behavior analysis* (the detailed social learning analysis of behavior) tells us what to do, what aspects of this youth's environment to help change, and (ultimately) how to change delinquent behavior. Behavioral assessment and analysis are presented in more depth in Chapter Three.

Recently, following this same ABC social learning model, the author has carried out a series of studies to determine just how another delinquent behavior (drinking alcohol) is learned (Stumphauzer, 1980a, 1980b; Stumphauzer & Perez, 1981). The following are twenty simple questions used to begin assessing precisely how adolescents learn to drink:

Antecedents

Setting Events

    1. Who is with you when you drink?
    2. Where does your drinking usually take place?

Modeling

    3. Did your friends drink before you did?
    4. Did you actually see them drink?
    5. Who are your favorite musicians?
    6. Do you think they use alcohol?

Self Control

    7. Is it wrong to use alcohol?
    8. Is it against the law to use or have alcohol?

Behavior

    9. Describe in detail how you usually use alcohol (circumstances, kind of alcohol, how much you drink, etc.).
    10. Describe in detail the last time you used alcohol.

Consequents

Drug Effects

    11. Does alcohol change the way you feel?
    12. In what way?
    13. Right after drinking, how do you feel?
    14. Later, like the next day, how do you feel?

Social Reinforcement

15. Right after drinking, do your friends approve?
16. Right after drinking, do your parents approve?
17. Later, like the next day, do your friends approve?

Self Control

18. Do you worry about health problems due to drinking?
19. Do you worry about being caught drinking?
20. What reason, if any, do you have for stopping drinking?

Together these studies strongly support the view that adolescent alcohol use follows social learning principles: it is modeled by peers, music "heroes," and (in some cases) family members; it is rewarded and reinforced both by drug effect (feel better, relax, etc.) and peer approval. Little in the way of self-control to lessen drinking was found.

8. BEHAVIOR CHANGE TECHNIQUES

Once we understand a particular teenager's delinquent behavior through an ABC assessment or behavior analysis, what is the most logical, effective, and ethical way to change it? It general, the very social learning influences found in our behavioral assessment to be "keeping the delinquent behavior going" need themselves to be changed. In addition, some new or infrequent behaviors may be taught "in place of" the delinquent behavior. That's it. Stop or alter some of the current events that are maintaining the crime, or teach a new, incompatible or "instead" behavior. Several social learning methods have been used effectively in the last ten years or so to help delinquents change and they will be described briefly here and presented in more detail in later chapters.

a. Institutional Programming

Social learning principles have been taught to the staff and corrections officers of institutions, and these principles have been applied in a variety of ways with confined youth. Rather than the traditional focus on the use of punishment, social learning approaches (such as token economies, behavioral contracting, and social skills training) have chiefly utilized positive, humane means to change behavior—modeling and reinforcement.

b. Behavioral Family Contracting

In this approach the focus is the whole family and a counselor negotiates a series of agreements or "contracts" on paper which act to give the family a structure often absent, to remove some of the stimuli and rewards for the delinquent behavior, and to teach "good," noncriminal "instead" behavior.

c. Social Skills Training

Either individually or in a group, the counselor quite deliberately teaches specific adaptive social behaviors often lacking in delinquents and incompatible with youth crime: assertion (standing up for their rights in a *nonaggressive* yet effective way), social problem solving, relating to authorities, etc.

d. Probation Contracting

Based on social learning principles, probation officers (together with the youth in trouble, the family, and perhaps the school) develop a very specific "contract" or agreement on paper spelling out exactly what behaviors will lead to release from probation and which will result in violation of probation and confinement. The new emphasis is on using nonpunitive principles like reward and modeling rather than the traditional focus on punishment.

e. School Programming

Social learning principles are applied to problems in school such as truancy, school achievement, theft, and aggression. The counselor may work directly with school personnel or through the youth and family on changing delinquent behavior in school.

f. Clinical Behavior Therapy

At times, delinquents are referred to professionals who try to work with delinquent behavior through regular office visits. Therapists have developed and utilized a series of methods in direct clinical treatment of delinquent behavior. These have included cognitive behavior therapy, self-control training, aversion therapy, cognitive sensitization, problem-solving, stress innoculation, and anger control training.

g. Employment Skills Training

Work, like other complex behaviors, has to be learned. Employment is especially a problem for youths labeled delinquent. Therefore, the focus of employment skills training is teaching youths precisely how to get and keep a job. Since employers and families are also important parts of the ABCs of jobs for these youths in trouble, they are also involved in the program. Natural reinforcements of employment (wages, praise, pride) are emphasized.

h. Group Treatment Homes

This approach utilizes "teaching parents" who are trained in social learning approaches to helping delinquents change in group homes set up specifically for small numbers of troubled youths. Essentially, social learning principles are applied to child rearing across the board: for learning family rules, for relating to "siblings," for learning self-control, for doing chores, for earning privileges, for school, and (ultimately) for returning to their natural home or for functioning independently.

i. Community Change and Prevention

Social learning principles are now being utilized directly where delinquent behavior is being learned: in the community itself. Rather than wait until youths are arrested and "forced" to change by the court, probation, the school, or the family, behavior change techniques are being applied in parks, on city streets, and in housing projects. On a broader scale, and perhaps most important, behavioral community psychology is working on *preventing* delinquent behavior. Some of the ABCs of delinquency can be changed in advance. Environmental design can range from something as ambitious as the design of a new community and the redesign of an "inner city" to something as simple as the addition of more lights on a particular street corner to prevent gang violence.

9. ADVANTAGES OF THE SOCIAL LEARNING APPROACH

What *are* the advantages of the social learning approach to helping delinquents change that has been described? There are several. First, as already has been discussed, the mystery is taken out of "understanding delinquency." This is accomplished by focusing on delinquent *behavior* and nondelinquent *behavior*. Second, rather than looking for "subconscious" causes or "early childhood trauma," this approach centers on the here-and-now of how delinquent behaviors are being learned and maintained *today*.

Third, the social learning approach applies measures of behavior that have use both in gauging progress of day to day change and in evaluating larger programs for changing delinquent behavior. This is a far cry from the use of traditional psychological tests (that conclude with relatively useless one-time scores on "psychopathy," "depression," and even "IQ") and also from psychiatric diagnosing and "pigeon holing" of youth into mental illness categories. The measures used in social learning approaches let you know what works and what doesn't, and in terms that make sense to families, schools, courts and (even) to teenagers.

Fourth, you will see that the social learning approach to changing delinquent behavior places a major emphasis on helping natural mediators (parents, teachers, neighbors) do the actual changing in the home, school and community. In addition, the youth is often engaged in determining goals and in changing his or her own behavior; in learning self-control, for example. This is in contrast to delinquent youths receiving "treatment" or "counseling," one hour a week which some people still believe will change behavior the remaining 167 hours in the week!

Fifth, it will become apparent that, for the most part, these approaches are humane, ethical, and positive in their focus on learning. This should prove a welcome change to our traditional non-humane, highly punitive, and even cruel attempts to change delinquent behavior—and this is especially important today with concern for basic human rights. Finally, sixth, the social learning approaches that you will be learning about can be evaluated and gradually improved so that we can eventually see some progress in this most challenging area.

10. RESISTANCE AND THE PROBLEMS OF COMPLIANCE

Many suggest that delinquents are especially difficult to work with—that they will resist change and often will not comply with counselling or treatment. "Resistance" in delinquent youths can take the form of refusal to attend meetings, oppositional statements, or even refusal to talk. Similarly, noncompliance can range from failure to do requested tasks to ''forgetting'' to bring in self-measures for the week.

A resistance to attend therapy sessions is often due to a fear of being viewed as ''crazy'' and a belief that ''these meetings will go on forever.'' These issues can be resolved in the first meeting with a discussion of ''we will focus on particular problems (in the family, etc.)'' and by using a contract specifying what will take place or time-limited approaches (''we will meet for ten times . . . and then *you* and your parents can decide whether to work on something else or not''). See Chapter Seven.

Resistance and noncompliance themselves, of course, can be broken down into specific behaviors (e.g., ''says 'no' to 60% of mother's requests,'' ''is late an average of 17 minutes for each session''). The antecedents (As) and consequences (Cs) that maintain these behaviors can then be examined and altered to increase compliance. The techniques of Forehand and McMahon (1981) in their book, *Helping The Noncompliant Child,* are especially helpful.

In the author's experience, the problems of resistance and noncompliance can often be avoided if the therapist forms an alliance with the youth—helping *him* choose goals and behaviors to work on, helping *her* voice her opinions in family meetings, and helping *him* get what he wants (e.g., to stay out late on Saturday nights) in exchange for a parental request (see Chapter Six on family contracting).

There may be further ''resistance'' from parents who are so angry that they cannot use positive reinforcement, but insist exclusively on the use of punishment. One technique is to focus first on a behavior that is a small compliance, relatively quick to improve, to model the use of praise, and to have parents practice it in the session. Another possibility would be anger control training for such parents (Chapter Ten).

SUMMARY

This chapter introduced the reader to the topic of juvenile delinquency and to ways to help delinquents change. Delinquency is extensive: more than two million young people a year are arrested for criminal behavior. Three types of theories of crime and delinquency were described: biological theories, social theories, and psychological theories. There is evidence that juvenile crime is not an all-or-none phenomena but rather exists along a continuum—from low frequency misconduct by almost every youth to severe and repetitious crime by relatively few serious offenders.

The chapter noted why arrest, juvenile justice, and probation do not seem to work. For any given youth, criminal behavior occurs at a low frequency and is inconsistently handled by the current system of arrest, court, and intervention too long after the behavior occurs. This sequence may actually reinforce the behavior the system is trying to ameliorate. The social learning approach can be summed up by: *delinquent behavior is acquired through psychological learning principles in a social context, and changing delinquent behavior requires application and variation of the same principles in a social context.*

The ABCs of delinquent behavior were described: antecedents (events before behavior) lead to criminal behaviors which are then maintained by consequents (various reinforcing events after the behavior). Car theft and alcohol use were presented as examples. Nine social learning approaches to helping delinquents change were introduced and are the topics of later chapters: institutional programming, behavioral family contracting, social skills training, probation contracting, school programming, clinical behavior therapy, employment skills training, group treatment homes, and community change for prevention. Six advantages of the social learning approach to helping delinquents change were delineated: mystery is removed, the here-and-now is the focus, measurement of change is incorporated, natural mediators (the youth, parents, teachers, neighbors) are utilized, the approach is nonpunitive and humane, and the social learning approach is consistent with program evaluation.

"Resistance" and noncompliance were discussed as behaviors to be specified, behaviorally analyzed, and addressed directly in helping delinquents change. The next chapter focuses on a behavioral analysis of nonproblematic youth and attempts to answer the question: why do some youths in high crime areas remain nondelinquent?

READINGS

1. Forehand, R. L., & McMahon, R. J. (1981). *Helping the noncompliant child: A clinician's guide to parent training.* New York: Guilford.

2. Stumphauzer, J. S. (1976). Modifying delinquent behavior: Beginnings and current practices. *Adolescence, 11,* 13–28.

3. Stumphauzer, J. S. (Ed.). (1979). *Progress in behavior therapy with delinquents.* Springfield, IL: Thomas.

CHAPTER 2

Understanding Nondelinquents:
The Forgotten Majority

1. THE FORGOTTEN MAJORITY?

It may seem unnecessary to devote a section of this book to nondelinquents—to young people who *don't* get in trouble. Why bother? What is the point? After all, our concern is with the others, with the delinquent youth who we must work with daily.

I believe it is absolutely necessary not only to have a general understanding of the concept of nondelinquency, but also to know precisely the social learning processes that result in nondelinquency. We don't yet have all the answers on how one youth becomes nondelinquent and another becomes a young criminal. We do have some of the answers. They will be the focus of this chapter.

A stress on nondelinquency is completely consistent with the social learning approach: if we better understand the "how to" of *not* getting into trouble, we would be in a much better position to help delinquents change, and also to *prevent* delinquent behavior. *In order for a delinquent to become a nondelinquent, they will have to learn these very skills.*

True, we seldom even think about "good" or nondelinquent teenagers. After all, they are no problem. The media (television news, newspapers and magazines) have not helped. Their focus is the sensational, the *un*usual, the attention grabbers and, too often, the young criminal. I mean, can you picture a headline:

"GHETTO YOUTH GETS JOB!"

Or, imagine hearing on television, "Teenager stays in school: stay tuned for film at 11:00!" This just doesn't happen. It wouldn't make money. Or would it? It hasn't really been tried.

Parents also neglect the "good kids" and many children learn that the only way to get attention from busy, preoccupied parents is to get in trouble. There is some truth to the old saying that "the wheel that squeaks the loudest gets the grease." This is certainly true in my experience over 15 years in child mental health clinics. I often ask parents two questions: "What does your child do that is good?" and "What do you do (what consequents) when they are good?" To the first question there is often silence as if they never even considered the good behavior. Then, frequently, they say "I don't do anything. I mean, we *expect* that." At times we see brothers and sisters begin to "act up" because the "bad one" in the family is getting all the attention.

How many nondelinquents are there? After reading in the newspapers about "youth crime wave" and "delinquency epidemic" you would think that nonproblem youth do not exist. In fact, they far outnumber delinquents and are the majority—albeit the forgotten majority. We recently researched an extremely high juvenile crime and youth-gang-dominated community and found, even there, that 75% of the youth were *not* in trouble with the police, the school, or with their families.

It would really help in our task here if we understood "how do they do it, how do they learn to stay out of trouble despite all the odds against them?" There has been considerable research on the topic. Some of the findings begin to answer this question.

2. STUDIES OF NONDELINQUENTS

Aiken (1981) has reviewed the psychological literature on nondelinquents. He found that most studies focused on nondelinquents chiefly as a *comparison* to delinquent youth. That is, clues to "unraveling delinquency" were sought in comparisons of young law breakers and young law abiders. A good deal of the research was a search for key family characteristics that result in "bad boys" or "good boys." West and Farrington (1973) produced a fund of information on who becomes delinquent and who becomes nondelinquent in England. The conclusions of a few studies that shed light on the particular characteristics of nondelinquents will be given here. Some of this research is nonbehavioral and some of these characteristics are inferred but a consensus seems to develop.

Pines (1979) concluded that what he termed "super kids" (those invulnerable to delinquency) shared some of the following characteristics:

1. extraordinary ability to respond to stress,
2. continue to develop in spite of deprivation,
3. at ease socially,
4. "immune" to bad influences,
5. know how to attract good adult influences,
6. have a high degree of independence,
7. skillful in whatever they do,
8. have a good relationship with at least one adult, and
9. may actually need challenges to keep them going.

In a classic study of the family relationships of 125 nondelinquent boys Reckless, Dinitz, and Murray (1957) found that parents of these nondelinquents exercise extensive supervision over their sons':

1. friendships,
2. leisure activities,
3. after school work,
4. movie attendance,
5. chores at home, and
6. general whereabouts at all times.

This group was followed-up four years later with largely the same results. Scarpitti, Murray, Dinitz, and Reckless (1960, p. 558) concluded

> At an average age of 16, these boys continue to assess themselves, their fathers, teachers, and schools favorably. They continue to isolate themselves from law-violating friends and acquaintances; they predict law-abiding behavior for themselves and, in this respect, they reflect their teachers' concepts of them . . . in sum, they continue to define themselves as good boys and are so defined by others in spite of remaining, for the most part, in high delinquency areas.

The need for parent involvement to prevent delinquency is further underscored by Fischer's review of parental supervision and delinquency. He concluded that "It seems clear that proper supervision of children is an effective means of reducing delinquency. What is needed now is to inform parents of its importance and to teach them the proper procedures for enhancing its effectiveness'' (Fischer, 1983, p. 639). He noted that parents of delinquent children rely substantially on punitive methods of control and lack consistent, positive childrearing practices. Fischer suggested that families of potential delinquents could benefit greatly from the several training packages available to assist in childrearing which emphasize positive child management techniques and, especially, the importance of parental supervision.

It has been suggested that delinquents are maladaptive, in part, simply because they lack the social skills to do better. In order to determine this, Freedman, Rosenthal, Donahoe, Schlundt, and McFall (1978) first developed an adolescent Problem Inventory of 44 items of problem situations facing today's teenagers to test the strengths and weaknesses in personal and interpersonal skills repertoires. These are two examples (Freedman et al., 1978, p. 1450 & 1452):

> You're visiting your aunt in another part of town, and you don't know any of the guys your age there. You're walking along her street, and some guy is walking toward you. He is about your size. As he is about to pass you, he deliberately bumps into you, and you nearly lose your balance. What do you say or do now?

> It is 1:30 at night, and you're walking along a street near your home. You're on your way home from your friend's home, and you know it is after curfew in your town. You weren't doing anything wrong. You just lost track of time. You see a patrol car cruising along the street and you feel scared, because you know you can get into trouble for breaking curfew. Sure enough, the car stops next to you, the policeman gets out, and he says, ''You there, put your hands on the car. Stand with your feet apart.'' What do you say or do now?

Next, a first validation study compared the social skills of institutionalized delinquent boys with ''leaders'' and ''good citizen students'' in a public high school and found the leaders to be most skilled, the ''good citizens'' next, and the delinquents least skilled. In a second study, Freedman et al. compared two groups of institutional delinquents with their social skill measure: one group who had frequent rule infraction and a second group with few problems in the institution. The low-problem group were found to be more socially skilled. Results can depend upon directions given and whether youths answer by multiple choice or free response. Based on these and other studies, social skill does seem a meaningful concept for understanding some of the differences between nondelinquents and delinquents. Also, this lends support to social skill training as one important technique for helping delinquents change (see Chapter Seven).

From the studies described above, we may begin to get a picture of nondelinquent child development, perhaps the beginning of a "recipe for nondelinquents." Unfortunately, there is presently much less information on nondelinquent girls. In one notable exception (Gaffney & McFall, 1981) it was found that social skills, expecially social skills in interacting with adult authority figures, were a key factor: nondelinquent girls were significantly more socially skilled than matched delinquent girls. Nondelinquent boys and girls develop a remarkable "invulnerability." Their parents are highly involved: they closely supervise their child's everyday life. Others view them as nondelinquent and they describe themselves as nondelinquent. They are more socially skilled. It might be more useful if we did a behavioral analysis of such nondelinquents. Exactly what good behavior do they have? How do they learn to be invulnerable, socially skilled nondelinquents?

3. CAESAR AND RICHARD: TWO BROTHERS AGAINST THE ODDS

In our community-based research of a youth gang (Stumphauzer, Aiken & Veloz, 1977), we came across two brothers who lived in the very same economically disadvantaged surroundings as the gang members, were members of the same ethnic minority, and had no father in their home to guide their development. The odds say they should have been delinquents. They were not. How is this possible? After all, they certainly fit the "multiple causation" theory for determining delinquency.

We agreed that there might be much to learn from them: how did they become nondelinquent, what exactly did they *do* to stay out of trouble, and could these "skills" be taught to other young people? The results are reported in detail elsewhere in a suggested reading (Aiken, Stumphauzer, & Veloz, 1977). We again utilized our behavior analysis approach to gain understanding of these two exceptional brothers:

A	B	C
What are the Antecedents; what stimulates or happens before nondelinquent behavior?	What exactly are the nondelinquent, trouble avoiding skills and Behaviors?	What are the Consequents; what does the nondelinquent behavior result in; what comes after that maintains it?

First of all we found that they *did not* keep out of trouble by staying at home or hiding, as many might think. They were quite active in their community and remained nondelinquent by getting to know gang members, police, and others. Then, they would assess any given "dangerous situation" and decide whether to try to change the situation or, as a last resort, to leave the scene. While there was no father in the home, an older neighbor (in fact, an ex-convict) had greatly influenced Caesar. He, in turn, taught Richard how to stay out of trouble. In addition, Caesar developed a highly rewarded skill (he restored cars) which was modeled and imitated by Richard (he restored bikes). Indeed, they seem to fit Pines' (1979) list of characteristics for "super kids." We discovered a comprehensive set of influences on them, of rewards and punishing consequents too.

What exactly were their behavioral assets (their good, nondelinquent behaviors), their behavioral excesses (potential problem behaviors they did too much), their behavioral deficits (behaviors they didn't do enough) their reinforcers, their punishers? These are summarized in Table 1. For example, they both were very careful to dress differently than gang members who they believed wore a sort of "uniform." In this way, by dressing what they called "normally," they learned not to be mistaken for gang members by either gangs or the police. Caesar could verbalize how he learned to drive through the community "like a snake," going where he wanted, yet avoiding especially dangerous corners and "trouble spots." He had learned that he could manipulate some situations (e.g., "talking a dude out of fighting"), but learned when to avoid other situations ("leave a party when troublemakers started getting loaded on alcohol and drugs"). Richard was picking up some of the same

Table 1

BEHAVIORAL ANALYSIS OF NONDELINQUENT BROTHERS

CAESAR	*RICHARD*
A. *BEHAVIORAL ASSETS*	
1. staying out of trobule	1. staying out of trouble
a. dress differently from *vatos*	a. dressing like older brother
b. know as many *vatos* as possible	b. know as many *vatos* as possible
c. self-control strategies	c. self-control strategies
d. model after *barrio counselor* ("Hood")	d. model after older brother (Caesar)
2. strong family relationships	2. strong family relationships
3. restores old cars	3. fixes bicycles
4. good work record	4. regular school attendance
5. articulate speaker	5. cultural and ethnic pride
6. cultural and ethnic pride	
B. *BEHAVIORAL EXCESSES*	
1. hangs around cliques' "alley"	1. hangs around cliques' "alley"
C. *BEHAVIORAL DEFICITS* (by own report)	
1. out of work	1. slow learner (reading and math)
2. not attending college	
3. not helping "homeboys" enough	
D. *MOST REINFORCING*	
1. *People:* immediate family *barrio counselor* ("Hood") girl friend	1. *People:* immediate family older brother (Caesar) "homeboys"
2. *Places:* home school movie theatre	2. *Places:* home movie theatre school
3. *Activities:* working on cars listening to music dating	3. *Activities:* working on bicycles reading comics going to dances
4. *Items:* cars books sports equipment	4. *Items:* bicycles cars camping equipment
5. *Social:* bing praised for a job well done	5. *Social:* being praised for hobbies

TABLE 1 (Continued)

CAESAR	RICHARD
being praised for a job well done being seen as warm and friendly being asked for advice	making others happy being told that he is right having others see him as a nice guy being asked for advice

E. *LEAST REINFORCING*

	CAESAR	RICHARD
1. *People:*	police store owners some neighbors	school teachers some neighbors
2. *Places:*	police station relatives' homes	school library police station
3. *Activities:*	drinking getting high and talking about "bad dudes"	drinking getting high and gambling school sports
4. *Items:*	rifles hats knives liquor tobacco pistols	liquor tobacco firearms knives uniforms some sports equipment
5. *Social:*	being famous and rich being seen as hard and tough being seen as a daredevil, *loco,* or as a guy who can hold his liquor	having others see him as cold and indifferent, crazy *(loco),* or as a guy who can hold his liquor

F. *PUNISHERS*

	CAESAR	RICHARD
1.	being in the wrong place at the wrong time	harassment at school by cliques
2.	fear of being shot, killed	harrassment by the police
3.	harrassment by the police	

skills from his model brother. He noted, for example, "when I walk into a store to buy ice cream, and there were gang members there that might hit me up for my money, I would say oh, I forgot my money, turn around, and leave." They had received a good deal of reinforcement for these behaviors—not only "success," but also praise from others and self-reinforcement ("I'm pretty good at this"). In addition both were active in keeping friends out of trouble: they were *teachers* of nondelinquency!

Questions remained. Were these two youths unique? Would similar nondelinquent behaviors and trouble avoiding skills be found in others in the same high-crime community?

4. NONDELINQUENTS ON THE MOVE

Wouldn't it be interesting if we could actually follow nondelinquents around day and night for a week to learn exactly what they do, who they are with, and how they stay out of trouble? This has actually been accomplished by Aiken (1981).

If we really followed them around and stood behind them, this itself would probably *change* the behavior. Psychologists call this "reactivity." Is there some less obtrusive way to follow them? If this were science fiction or a James Bond movie we could use "brain implants" or some complex electronic tracking system. Aiken actually did utilize a common and omnipresent electronic system—the "beeper" or paging device.

Ten teenagers were selected who were not delinquent but did meet the "multiple causation" theory of delinquency (minority status, low income, high juvenile crime community, *and* had a brother identified as a delinquent). They were each given an electronic paging device and were "beeped" on a random schedule seven different times a day for one week. When "beeped" they were to record where they were, who they were with, what they were doing, how rewarding and challenging it was, and if they were "forced to" or "free to" do whatever it was.

It appears as though these youths were mainly "trouble avoiders." When "beeped" the majority were at home with family members and, quite frequently, watching television. This is perhaps the safest of alternatives in a high juvenile crime community. In fact, we asked Caesar in the previous study how could a kid stay out of trouble in this same community if he had to. His reply "He'd have to go in his house when the sun went down and lock the door!" The next most frequent behaviors of these nondelinquents were some form of active recreation with friends or talking with friends. For the most part, they did all these things without coercion; the exception was "had to" go to school.

In general they reported few alternatives to choose from; there was little challenge in or reinforcement for these nondelinquent behaviors. This is perhaps a sad commentary on youth in our economically disadvantaged communities where there are not many choices—even more true today with cutbacks in recreation and community development programs. As Caesar cogently put it "there are all kinds of programs for kids who get in trouble but none for the ones who don't."

Some youths do learn to avoid trouble and quietly pursue the few alternatives provided them. Others, "super kids" like Caesar and Richard, go out and apparently make alternatives. They are seemingly guided by a "significant other" model and do find rewards for not only avoiding trouble but also for social skills like assertiveness and giving help. Dealing with the pressure to drink alcohol and abuse drugs is related to these findings.

5. LEARNING NOT TO DRINK

After completing a behavior analysis research series on teenagers who were learning to drink (Stumphauzer, 1980a) the author decided to extend the study along the nondelinquent dimension presented above. We conducted behavior analysis (ABC) interviews with 100 adolescents who were abstainers to see how they were learning *not* to drink (Stumphauzer, 1983). Possible clues to *prevention* of alcohol and drug abuse were sought.

The antecedents ("A") of not drinking were of interest. The effect of modeling by a significant other was again critical. Thirty-five percent of these teenagers looked up to somebody special who did not drink. In addition, a substantial percentage of their parents did not drink: 45% of their fathers and 69% of their mothers. While some of their friends did drink, for the most part they did not pressure these youths to drink.

"Non-drinking behaviors" ("B") were chiefly of two kinds. First, there were the social skills involved in saying "no" to peer pressures to drink: assertion ("No, I just don't want it"). Second, there were alternative or "instead" behaviors: spending time with nondrinking friends, keeping busy with other activities, and general "nondrug" beliefs ("I just get high on life and don't need drugs").

Finally, the results or consequences ("C") were compliments from others and, perhaps more important, self-reinforcement (self statements of pride and accomplishment). This is a new twist in the drug abuse literature—learning from people who are abstaining and exerting natural self-control. It would seem promising to utilize these youths who have learned *not* to abuse alcohol and drugs as "peer-teachers" in preventative programs.

6. NONDELINQUENTS: A PRELIMINARY FORMULATION

What have we learned from the behavior analysis of nondelinquents? What have these various studies taught us about "how do youth learn to stay out of trouble?" Some of the aspects of nondelinquency may be beyond our immediate control for generally teaching this cluster of abilities. There may not be ideal models for every child; there certainly are not ample alternatives to youth crime in all communities (jobs, recreation, opportunities to help other youths, etc.). It is difficult to limit or minimize exposure to delinquent models (from criminal peers to violent superstars in television, music, and movies). But there are determinable social skills that can be taught and some of these will be presented in Chapter Seven. These skills can be taught to youths already in trouble to *change* delinquent behavior, or they can be taught generally to children to *prevent* delinquent behavior.

We don't have all the answers yet, but we do have some of them. Let us summarize with a preliminary formulation on the social learning of nondelinquency based on our various research projects:

1. Nondelinquents are strongly guided (taught) by at least one family member, *or* substitute significant other, who not only demonstrates or models productive, noncriminal behavior, but also reinforces or rewards it in the youth.
2. Nondelinquents learn, either from a model or by trial-and-error, a set of social skills:
   a. assertiveness to say "no" to delinquent peer influence and drugs/alcohol use;
   b. finding other *non*delinquent friends;
   c. conversation skills;
   d. finding and utilizing alternative sources of reward and reinforcement (including self-statements of pride and accomplishment); and
   e. if all else fails, learn how to avoid situations with a high probability of trouble, or to leave the scene as they see trouble developing.

SUMMARY

This chapter introduced the reader to the topic of non-delinquents—youth who do *not* get in trouble. An understanding of the social learning processes that result in nondelinquent (or even prosocial) behavior may not only aid in helping delinquents change, but also help prevent delinquency from developing. It is consistent with the thesis of this book that *young people can and do learn a set of social skills that keep them out of trouble.*

A number of studies have focused on nondelinquents or even "superkids" who, despite social disadvantages of poverty, broken homes, and high-crime communities, do something remarkable: they excell! Some found that parents or others exerted a strong influence. Other research has supported the idea that nondelinquents are more socially skilled than delinquents.

For example, two brothers who lived in a high juvenile crime neighborhood dominated by gang violence were behaviorally analyzed by the author and colleagues. They were found to be assertive, they learned nondelinquent behavior, were strongly influenced by an exconvict neighbor, and had behaviors alternative to crime that were strongly reinforced (restoring cars and bicycles).

The chapter concluded with a preliminary formulation of nondelinquency. Nondelinquents are strongly influenced in a noncriminal direction (taught through modeling and shaping) by a significant other. Parental supervision may play an important role. Nondelinquents learn a set of social skills: assertiveness to say "no" to delinquent peer influences, they find and are influenced by nondelinquent friends, they find reinforcement for productive noncriminal behavior, and they learn when to leave or avoid a potentially troublesome situation.

The next chapter takes up the complex and varied evaluation of delinquent behavior. Behavioral assessment is offered as an alternative to traditional psychological testing and assessment reports.

READINGS

1. Aiken, T. W., Stumphauzer, J. S., & Veloz, E. V. (1977). Behavioral analysis of nondelinquent brothers in a high juvenile crime community. *Behavioral Disorders, 2,* 212–222.

2. Stumphauzer, J. S. (1983). Learning not to drink: Adolescents and abstinence. *Journal of Drug Education, 13,* 39–48.

3. West, D. J., & Farrington, D. P. (1973). *Who becomes delinquent?* London: Heinemann Educational.

CHAPTER 3

Evaluation:
Assessing the Behavior of Delinquents

As we have seen, the behavior of both delinquents and nondelinquents can be understood or "figured out" with a social learning analysis. But where does the therapist, counselor, or probation officer actually begin when faced with a real, live delinquent? Where should one start? How do you organize the information available to you in the most useful manner? What treatment or intervention strategy should be selected? The answer is to begin with a behavioral analysis of the particular youth, his or her immediate surroundings and the current influences on their behavior (Mash & Terdal, 1981). Obviously, it will be important and necessary to focus on behaviors which are of concern to (a) the law, (b) the family, (c) the school, and (d) the youth himself or herself. As you will see, assessing *delinquent* behavior presents some particular problems, but they are not insurmountable.

1. WHY BEHAVIORAL ASSESSMENT?

A detailed, social learning assessment is absolutely necessary before you can proceed to helping delinquents change. Your assessment will tell you what the problems are, what and who is currently maintaining them, which change strategy logically follows, and how effective your program is.

Craighead, Kazdin, and Mahoney (1981) have described four important characteristics of behavioral assessment that will be further explained below in light of helping delinquents change:

a. *Behavioral assessment provides an understanding of the problem.* As you have already seen, the social learning approach shifts from a focus on "delinquency" to the

31

behavior of delinquents—the ABCs (antecedents, behavior, and consequents). While a subtle shift, the result is behavior we can understand, measure, and change. If "theft in the classroom" is found to be stimulated by "purses being left on desks" and reinforced by buying snacks and attention from usually *un*attentive parents, then we have made considerable progress in understanding the problem. Unlike traditional assessments such as psychological tests which result in relatively useless scores, behavior analysis has direct and continuing utility.

b. *Behavioral assessment provides information for the development of a treatment plan.* In the example above the choices for changing the delinquent stealing behavior are quite obvious: (a) change the environment; make the purses less available, (b) remove some of the reinforcements for stealing, (c) replace reinforcement with punishment, (d) help parents give attention for good behavior, or (e) some combination of these. In addition, in a behavior analysis one gathers information on the motivations/incentives in the family and the social context in which change must take place. What are the *youth's* motivations? What will his friends do if he starts changing his behavior?

c. *Behavioral assessment emphasizes the current level of functioning.* Rather than look for "hidden causes" in early childhood, the social learning approach to assessment focuses largely on the "here and now:" this last week in school, last weekend at home, yesterday, *this morning.* While all problems do have a "history" (some a long history), these behaviors are currently maintained by recent events. These events (the events today and tomorrow) must be changed. The "here and now" will change as treatment or counseling progresses. A behavioral family contract drawn up two weeks ago may well need to be adjusted today, now that school is out, for example.

d. *Behavioral assessment is continuous throughout treatment.* Traditional assessments like psychological tests or psychiatric "mental status" evaluations are typically carried out once and some speculation is made about the "causes" of the delinquency. In behavioral assessment measures are on-going throughout intervention or treatment to assess progress and provide feedback on what is working and not working. This more scientific, experimental design of assessment-intervention-assessment-intervention is one of the major contributions of social learning to the therapy and counseling field.

Usually, the first session or two will be utilized for the initial behavioral assessment. A good deal of information will be gathered from the youth, his family, and from school and court records. In addition, the behavioral analysis will incorporate: (a) an initial interview with the youth and family, (b) direct observation and (c) usually the development of specialized measures of the particular problems at hand—e.g., daily report card for school, self-measurement of "number of times angry" and the circumstances (ABCs), and family routines ("nights came in on time"). Finally, the behavioral analysis will result in a synthesis of information: a social learning analysis of the delinquent behavior, an intervention plan, and a method for measuring and reflecting progress in changing delinquent behavior.

There are some special problems in assessing delinquent behavior. Unlike other clients, delinquents are usually *not* the ones seeking help. Often they are quite content with the way things are— except perhaps for being "caught" or currently being "in trouble." Commonly, they will say there is "no problem." Very often they are seen by counselors or in clinics because *others* (parents, teachers, the court) want them to change. As noted in Chapter One, they will be more cooperative if they take part in the decision of what to measure, if they are reinforced for compliance, and if the therapist establishes an alliance ("I'll help *you* get off probation and see that *you* get to speak up in family meetings . . . ").

2. DEFINING BEHAVIORS

It is necessary to define behaviors in objective, descriptive terms so that they can be accurately recorded and then assessed (Ollendick & Hersen, 1984). The general rule of thumb is that the behaviors must be observable (rather than inferred) so that people (parents, youth, the court) agree if they occur or not and, preferably, that each behavior be one that can be counted. As you will see, some effort at initial meetings to define and specify behaviors will not only aid your behavioral assessment, but will help the often overwhelmed family begin to focus on discrete behaviors that can be understood and changed. The following are a few examples of generalities or inferred behaviors on the left that are redefined as specific behaviors on the right:

GENERALITIES	SPECIFIC BEHAVIORS
"bad attitude"	"says 'no' to father's requests 60% of time"
"bugs sister"	"calls sister fat and pulls sister's hair"
"always comes home late"	"late an average of 30 minutes"
"cuts school"	"absent 6 days last month"
"a thief"	"took $5.00 and then $10.00 from mother's purse last month"

3. THE INITIAL INTERVIEW

In most counseling or treatment settings the first contact with a youth with delinquent behaviors will take the form of an interview, a face-to-face meeting, and should include his or her family as well. While you may have some information before hand (reports from probation, school, or other referral source), you will need to pursue other pertinent information directly. There are five main goals of the initial interview: (a) together with the youth and family to organize information and come to some understanding of the problem(s), (b) to give information regarding the counseling or treatment you or your clinic have to offer, (c) to assess the appropriateness of seeing this youth or the need for referral elsewhere (to a neurologist, to a hospital, etc.), (d) to assess motivation of the youth and parents, and (e) to come to a preliminary agreement with the teenager and family about what exactly you will be doing together (goals, methods, time limits, etc.).

Before seeing the family, perhaps while they are waiting in the waiting room, it is often a good idea to have one or both parents fill out a questionnaire or checklist. In Table 2 you will find Clement's "Parent's Evaluation of Child's Behavior." You will find it useful and time-saving in that it rapidly gives you information on how the parent conceptualizes the problem(s), and it orients the parents to thinking about specific behaviors and the circumstances under which they occur (ABCs) even before you see the family.

Table 2

PARENTS EVALUATION OF CHILD'S BEHAVIOR

Paul Clement, Ph.D.
Fuller Graduate School
Of Psychology

Child's Name_____ Age_____

Parent's Name_____ Date_____

In order to aid your psychological consultant in being of maximal help to you, please answer the questions on the following pages.

BEHAVIORAL EXCESSES

What does your child do too often, too much, or at the wrong times that gets him into trouble? List all the behaviors that you can think of.

1._____
2._____
3._____
_____

BEHAVIORAL DEFICITS

What does your child fail to do as often as you would like, as much as you would like, or when you would like?

1._____
2._____
3._____
_____

BEHAVIORAL ASSETS

What does your child do that you like? What does he do that other people like?

1._____
2._____
3._____
_____

GOALS

What do you hope to accomplish as a result of your working with the psychological consultant? What behaviors from page 1 do you want to see changed and how much must they change for you to be satisfied?

_____
_____
_____
_____

Now please list the one behavioral excess from page 1 and the one deficit from page 1 which you most want to see changed first.

excess: _____
deficit: _____

During the first session one needs to assess any immediate needs such as an upcoming court date, the next meeting with the probation officer, getting the youth back into school, or settling any other crisis that cannot wait until later. Often, you the mediator, can help balance such a crisis by exploring the alternatives out loud with the whole family (perhaps for the first time!) and let them come to a decision. This may be important for setting the tone for further negotiations in behavioral family contracting (Chapter Six).

The initial interview is often split between seeing the whole family at first and then the adolescent alone and finally all together again. This may take one to two hours. Since the family is frequently the focus of change it is well to begin together. The delinquent behavior did not develop in a vacuum and the family is often maintaining the behavior—even in subtle ways such as giving attention only when he or she is in trouble. Also, by sharing the responsibility for problems with the family, the youth is not made the "bad guy" and it is less likely that he or she will be resistant or alienated from cooperating in any subsequent program. This is especially important in working with delinquent youths because they may be coming to the initial interview "against their will" to begin with. Indeed, the parents may well have some investment in keeping the problem "the kid's problem." Many parents would be only too happy for the "doctor to fix it" or for a pill to make the problem go away. Seeing the family together will help in their sharing responsibility—if not for the problems, at least for some of their solutions.

It is well to let family members (including the youth) present the problems in general terms, and then to go after specifics: the As (antecedents), Bs (specific behaviors) and Cs (consequents).

You might begin with questions like "Why are you here? What problems have you been having?" This allows anyone in the family to respond and to express problems in their own terms. You can then pursue specific problem behaviors with statements like "tell me more about. . . . " Family members often describe behaviors in generalities ("well, you know, they fight"). You can get them to be both more specific and to begin thinking about discrete behaviors by asking "What did they actually *do*?" In order to get information on life in the home I often ask them to "please describe a typical day in the family from the time the first family member gets up to when the last goes to bed." While this isn't direct observation it often results in information in family routine and interactions that you would otherwise miss. Another thing I do if a family is having difficulty in describing a particular problem, if they are being too abstract, is to ask them to "describe in detail the *last time* it occurred: how did it start (A), who did what (B) and then what happened after (C), what was the result?"

An alternative way to go after antecedents (those events that lead up to or stimulate the problem behavior) is to ask "what was happening the half hour before?" Similarly, for consequents (those events that follow or reinforce the behavior), "what took place the half hour after?" While you may get "well, she was punished, I sent her to her room." You may find that in her room she plays records and uses her telephone!

In pursuing antecedents, specific behaviors, and consequents with the family or youth in the first session you will be showing them, quite directly, how to understand the problems in the family, what may be maintaining them, and what needs to be altered to change the delinquent behavior. This removes any mystery about "how could this happen?" Later, together, you can review this social learning conceptualization of the problem(s) and the then more logical interventions available.

Another aspect of this approach that you will start in the initial interview is the topic of measurement. "How many times did this happen?" "How long did it go on, how many minutes?" "How often did it occur last week—do you all agree with that?" Sometimes there are records to give this information and the family should be engaged in reviewing them. "The school record says she was absent 30 days last semester." "The probation report states he was arrested four times last year under the influence of alcohol or drugs." These beginning points of measurement may be clarified and you can request the family, youth, or school to record specific behaviors beginning the week after the initial session and continuing throughout treatment: "I'd like you to keep track of these things on this card during this week, and to bring it to the next session. On the first line we'll measure when he comes home each night, just write in the time. On the second line simply write the number of family arguments, if any, each day."

It is suggested to see the adolescent alone as well, after the family meeting. I believe this is especially important with delinquents. Often they feel "ganged up on" by the family, police, and the therapist too. Also, frequently they will not talk during the family session and act like "the accused." It is paramount to gain their cooperation and motivation in changing. One can begin with a fairly loose statement like "what did you think about all that? Is that the way you see it too?" It may help to focus on the larger system than just the youth: "It looks like there are several problems in the family (school, neighborhood) and not just yours." "What do *you* think needs to be changed?" Indeed, it may be necesary to side with the adolescent in order to balance the family enough to come to agreements to work on problems: "You know I agree with you—it's not all your problem and I'm willing to say that when we meet again, to be on *your* side."

Aside from gaining rapport and a working alliance with the teenager alone, you might need to pursue information directly from them about the ABCs of their behavior. It is also useful in gaining rapport to pursue their assets: "what do you like to do best, what are you good at, and what are you proud of?" While alone with the adolescent, a survey of their incentives (rewards and reinforcers) and punishers is suggested as they may be incorporated in motivating behavior change. In Table 3 you will find the author's twenty item "Favorite Things Survey." The youth can be asked to fill it out or you can give it as an interview.

At the end of the initial session you can see the whole family together again to wind things up. It is best to give some kind of summary statement about the specifics of the problem behaviors presented and a brief social learning formulation about what appears to be maintaining them. It is wise to include some supportive statement about the adolescent's cooperation and positive behaviors. Then ask for their feedback regarding its accuracy (include the youth). After a discussion of this you can briefly present a plan for treatment or counseling that logically follows from the formulation just given. Seek, and further discuss if necessary, their agreement to take part. Once this initial "treatment contract" is achieved, get down to the specifics of when the next meeting will be, who will be involved, and any "homework" for them to do in the meanwhile (measurement, etc.). Releases for information may be acquired at this time, especially if you will need to talk to teachers, probation officers, etc. In fact, if behavior problems are occurring in school, you may want to interview the teacher or observe behavior directly in the classroom (Atkeson & Forehand, 1981).

Table 3

FAVORITE THINGS SURVEY

Jerome S. Stumphauzer, Ph.D.
University of Southern California
School of Medicine

Name_____ Date_____

1. Who is your favorite relative?

2. What do you like to do most with them?

3. Who is your favorite teacher? Your faviorite subject?

4. When you do something good, what does your mother do?

5. When you do something good, what does your father do?

6. When you do somethig good in school, what do your teachers do?

7. When you do something bad, what does your father do?

8. When you do something bad, what does your mother do?

9. When you do something bad in school, what do your teachers do?

10. If someone just gave you five dollars, what would you do with it?

11. If you had a chance, what would you like to do most of all?

12. What is the worst punishment your parents use on you?

13. Does it work?

14. What would you like to earn?

15. Where would you like to go for a day, and who would you like to take with you?

16. What are your five favorite TV programs?

    1.
    2.
    3.
    4.
    5.

17. What are your five favorite foods?

    1.
    2.
    3.
    4.
    5.

TABLE 3 (Continued)

```
18. Who are your five best friends?

    1.
    2.
    3.
    4.
    5.

19. Who punishes you the most?   How?

20. What five things would you like to have, that you don't have
now?

    1.
    2.
    3.
    4.
    5.
```

4. DIRECT OBSERVATION

There are limits to interviews. While you do observe the youth and his family directly when they are speaking, they are often giving you a verbal report of what took place. The information, therefore, is based on their memory of events and on their ability to observe and report what they experienced. Also, they may have reasons to distort what they report: to "look good," to only tell part of the story, or even to present things as worse than they are. While interviews are necessary, and are the first step in beginning to help delinquents change, they are not sufficient in themselves to assess behavior and the circumstances surrounding the behavior. Already noted above was the additional use of measures that the family or youth may be asked to keep during the week, and to bring to the next session. In addition, direct observation may be useful.

A type of assessment that is somewhere between the interview and observing directly in the natural environment is the simulated situation. For example, while interviewing the family about how the last argument developed you might simply ask them to "role play" right there in the office: "show me what happened, just like it was, start it off just like at home, and everybody do the same thing." Another way to use simulated situations is to utilize an observation room with a one-way window if available. If two siblings often fight over games, have them play a game while you observe. If it is a problem between teenager and parents, give them ten minutes to discuss it: "I'm going to leave you in this room for ten minutes and I'd like you to discuss curfew hours for Junior." "Try to act just like you would at home."

Direct observation may be the most enlightening, but has some of its own problems. Observation can be carried out by a trained observer, yourself, a teacher, or a member of the family. You or another trained observer would be in a good position to observe and record the specific behaviors and the "befores" and "afters." However, the behavior may not occur at all under observation—especially delinquent or criminal behavior! The presence of an observer can change the environment of the home or school and, therefore, the behavior of everyone. Still, many following the social learning approach have successfully utilized direct observation. Family interactions can be observed directly as can various social skills, rates of "looking at person speaking," responses to praise, etc. Patterson, Reid, Jones, and Conger (1975), in their work with families of aggressive children routinely observe families in the home for six evenings at the beginning (baseline period) and again three, six, and twelve months after treatment "to be sure the things you wanted changed really did change." They use a set of seven rules for families they will observe:

a. Everyone in the family must be present.
b. No guests should be present during observations.
c. The family is limited to two rooms in order to allow the observer to view all family members.
d. The observers' time schedule allows them to wait only 10 minutes for all family members to be present in the two rooms.
e. Telephone: no calls out; answer incoming calls briefly.
f. No television viewing.
g. No conversations with observers while they are coding.

Patterson and others have developed fairly complicated methods of observing and coding the behavior of families that have been useful in demonstrating change in families due to social learning treatment. There are some drawbacks to these systems: they are time consuming, costly, and observers must be highly trained. Another common approach is the time sample in which one observes for ten seconds and then records persons and behaviors during the next twenty seconds and continues in this manner. Johnson, Christensen, and Bellamy (1976) have also developed a system for sending home a tape recorder system with families being evaluated. It can be played during dinner time, for example, and in this way fairly unobtrusively "observe" or record typical family interactions.

Of course, direct observation is also possible in the classroom if that is an important arena of behavior and if the school will cooperate. It is my experience that they usually do, especially since delinquent behavior in the school is their problem too (see assessing school problems below). Percentage of time on-task, number of times out of seat, number of interruptions, number of fights, etc., can be measured.

Delinquent behavior often does not occur in the home or school, it happens out with friends, on streets, in stores, and in parks. While difficult, it is possible to observe directly in the community. For instance, we did accomplish this in our social learning studies of youth gangs (Stumphauzer, Aiken & Veloz, 1977). While making home visits and family observations, I have asked the problem youth to show me around the neighborhood: "Show me where you spend your time," "are any of your friends around, I'd like to meet them."

Of course there is one observer who is always there watching: when delinquent behaviors and "good" behaviors are happening— the youth him or herself. Often you can gain their cooperation in measuring behavior and reporting it. Aiken (1981) utilized electronic paging devices to "beep" youth in the community as a signal to record where they were and what they were doing. Naturally, there may be reasons to distort or not tell it like it really was. While time consuming and possibly costly, more than one observation approach might be the best choice for accurate assessment.

5. ASSESSING CRIMINAL BEHAVIOR

Criminal behavior is especially difficult to measure and assess. By its very nature, if it is successful, it goes undetected! Nobody saw it, and the criminal is not going to volunteer that they did it because they will get in trouble. A second problem is that, quite often, criminal behavior is a low-frequency behavior—it only happens rarely or occasionally or, perhaps, only once. A youth may only commit a serious crime like armed robbery once, be caught, arrested, and it may not occur again. Generally, for any given youth, the more serious the crime the less frequent. Shop lifting or truancy may be more frequent than armed assault. In addition, with children and teenagers, there are two kinds of delinquent behaviors.

There are "capital offenses" which are offenses that would also be crimes for adults (theft, assault, etc.). But there are also "status offenses" which are offenses only for youths (truancy, curfew violation, and incorrigibility, for example). Here we will focus mainly on assessing crime or capital offenses. In spite of the problems outlined above, crime *is* measurable. In this section four ways of assessing or measuring criminal behavior will be discussed: official police reports, direct observation, unobtrusive measures, and self-report.

Chances are if you are assessing a delinquent you already have some kind of "official" report from police or probation that lists the occurrences when this youth committed particular crimes. Police do apprehend youths committing crimes and record this in official reports. Probation reports usually go into some detail in documenting the history and circumstances of crimes and status offenses of each youth they evaluate. But this is official crime, and the problem is that a great deal of delinquent behavior goes undetected and unrecorded by police. Sometimes, even though "minor" crimes are detected by police, they handle them "unofficially" and do not report them. This, as research shows, is especially true if the youth is a girl and/or an affluent, non-minority member. However, police records *are* important. Indeed, they may determine a youth's future: whether he or she gets "put away" or not, stays in school or not, is removed from probation or not, and even gets a job or not. Too often, treatment programs for delinquents use police reports as the only measure of success. They are *one* important measure, and one which you may certainly want to incorporate in your assessment. You may need a "release of information" from parents to get these reports or regular information and cooperation from police or from the youth's probation officer. I might also add that "number of arrests" does not necessarily have anything to do with number of convictions or guilt. While this may seem obvious, with teenagers, "number of arrests" is often treated as an indication of how much trouble they have been in, guilty or not. Use police and probation reports in your continuing assessment of delinquent behavior, but not as the only measure. Police reports do "make the most sense" and are "the bottom line" to community funding sources, schools, and juvenile courts, and even for parents.

As mentioned earlier, direct observation of crime is difficult but not always impossible. Banks and stores now have video cameras and one way viewing screens. Children and teenagers are fairly closely observed in some settings like school and the home, and sometimes in stores and parks. Some families and teachers, for example are quite capable of recording theft, fighting, vandalism. As you may find in your initial interview, parents can report things like "Oh, I'd say she fights at least two times a week." In the case of stealing reported earlier (Stumphauzer, 1976b), I used the *Daily Behavior Card* found in Figure 2 to assess stealing in school and at home by asking the teacher and parents to record daily. The same can be accomplished with other common delinquent behaviors. Keep in mind that not all of crime will be recorded, but you can get a fair assessment of crime by carefully instructing your observers, checking their accuracy, and by using more than one means of assessment.

Direct observation, as discussed earlier, can be obtrusive: the observation itself can alter the environment and, therefore, change behavior. *Un*obtrusive measures are those that don't intrude. For example, department stores take inventory and can tell how much shoplifting has taken place. While unobtrusive, they cannot tell *who* took what. In the home, however, if money is repeatedly missing from the cookie jar, the thief can be narrowed down pretty quickly! If you keep leaving two dollars in change every day you can assess how much is missing and when the stealing stops. At school, for example, it is usually not to hard to find out whose graffitti is on the wall. So, unobtrusive measures of crime at home and school are possible and might be utilized as one measure, depending on your creativity in developing such assessments.

Finally, there is self-report. It may seem ridiculous to ask a delinquent to record his own crimes! Also, you may expect "resistance" in keeping records. In my experience, however, this is sometimes possible, especially when (a) there is some motivation to change, (b) they are also asked to record pleasant or good behavior, and (c) when they are being rewarded (even paid) to do it. Perhaps amazingly, your attention alone is often enough to reinforce record keeping. Some probationers in the groups social skills program outlined in Chapter Seven have asked if they could use the Daily Behavior Card for another week! You may want to ask the youth and some other observer to *both* record the same behavior and then check their accuracy and level of agreement before relying on one or the other. This is what I found in the same case of stealing mentioned above. The twelve year old girl agreed to measure "number of times I steal" at home, at school, and at the store. Her

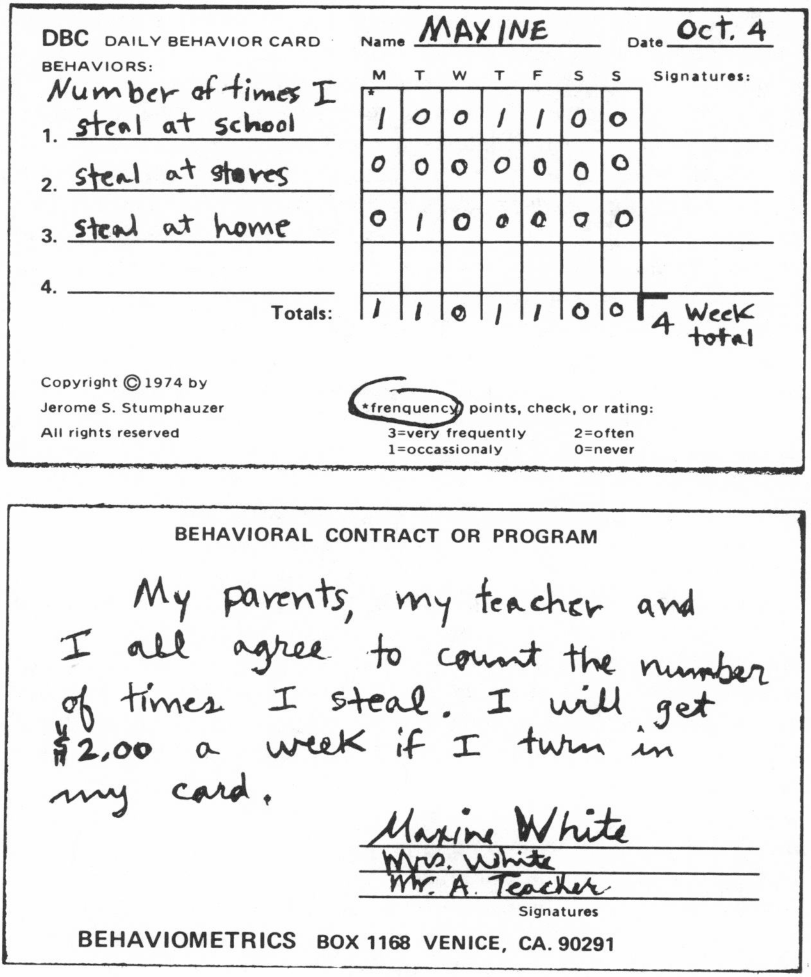

DBC DAILY BEHAVIOR CARD	Name MAXINE						Date Oct. 4	

BEHAVIORS:

Number of times I

	M	T	W	T	F	S	S	Signatures:
1. steal at school	1	0	0	1	1	0	0	
2. steal at stores	0	0	0	0	0	0	0	
3. steal at home	0	1	0	0	0	0	0	
4.								
Totals:	1	1	0	1	1	0	0	4 Week total

Copyright © 1974 by
Jerome S. Stumphauzer

*frenquency points, check, or rating:

3=very frequently   2=often
1=occassionaly   0=never

BEHAVIORAL CONTRACT OR PROGRAM

My parents, my teacher and I all agree to count the number of times I steal. I will get $2.00 a week if I turn in my card.

Maxine White
Mrs. White
Mr. A. Teacher
Signatures

BEHAVIOMETRICS BOX 1168 VENICE, CA. 90291

FIGURE 2. Daily Behavior Card.

figures did agree with those of her parents and the teacher. In fact, while gaining self-control of her stealing, *she* suggested changing the measures into her own words. Another self-measurement device that children and adolescents are especially willing to use because it is "fun" is the "wrist behavior counter" (a simple, inexpensive frequency counter they wear like a watch). "Resistance" and noncompliance can be minimized if the youth helps choose which behaviors to count, assesses some behaviors that they like (e.g., "number of times played baseball") and if they are reinforced for self-report measures (e.g., allowance in exchange for completed Daily Behavior Card). Hindelang, Hirschi, and Weis (1981) have developed a self-report form for measuring relatively minor crimes; it can be found in Chapter Seven. Self-report, or self-measurement, in fact, is the first step in Kanfer and Karoly's (1972) three level model of learning self-control: (a) self-assessment (counting), (b) self-evaluation (noting to yourself how you are doing), and (c) self-reinforcement ("I'm proud of myself!"). Since self-control is certainly one of the goals here, you would do well to incorporate some form of self-assessment for the youth in changing their own delinquent behavior.

6. ASSESSING FAMILY PROBLEMS

If changing delinquent behavior is your goal, assessing crime is only one aspect of the total picture. As already noted, what goes on in the family, school and community has a great deal to do with delinquent behavior. You may well want to assess other areas of family functioning besides the criminal behavior of the one child.

One method, already mentioned, is direct observation of the family at home. Cues to general family conflict other than the identified client's problems may become obvious. You may find, for example, that no one in the family gets any positive attention, and that the only time anyone is noticed is if they have a problem. You may discover what Patterson (1982) has termed the "coercive family." In these families children engage in excessive rates of behaviors that upset their parents. The parents, in turn, retaliate with excessive rates of aversive or punishing responses. And the cycle continues. In fact, it is quite common to find that there is an excessive (almost exclusive) use of punishment in the families of delinquents (Stuart, 1970). Another simple method of assessing families that I use is to ask the family to keep a "diary" or record of what happened in the family for the whole week between the initial assessment session and second session.

Key areas of possible family problems should be assessed. This can be accomplished with a simple checklist: each parent and the child can check off any of the areas that they believe are problems in their family. An especially important area is the use of discipline in the family. Are directives and guidelines given to the children? Who responds when they are not met? Who (if anyone) responds when they *are* met? What discipline is used: scolding, loss of love, physical punishment, "grounding?" Under what circumstances does each work or not work? Are any incentives used for good behavior? Is there any evidence or history of child abuse in the family? How do the children control their parents? Are there any family rules? Often, in families of delinquents, there are no set family rules or agreements regarding things like curfew, knowledge of whereabouts, knowledge of who the child is with, etc. Chapter Two noted the importance of parental supervision. Are there major disputes between the children and, if so, over what? Is there a major marital problem in the parents? If it is a "one parent home," is there any appropriate role model for the child? Is money a problem in the family? How do the children get money or the things they want? Is there an allowance, and is it "earned" or given regardless of behavior? Once problem areas are discovered and discussed with the family, they may be incorporated in the current counseling (they may need to be if directly related to the delinquent behavior) or they may be worked on separately (marital counseling, for example). The problems can be further assessed by direct observation, a simulated or "role play" session, or by the family members involved in keeping track of them with some simple counting procedure on a Daily Behavior Card.

7. ASSESSING SCHOOL PROBLEMS

Delinquents are all school age, and most do attend school (See Chapter Nine). It will come as no surprise that their delinquency may include the time they spend at school. Therefore, assessment of behavior *in* school can become an important part of your program. In addition, success in school is a major component of *non*delinquent behavior and may be a goal in changing delinquent behavior.

You may well have a report from the school in front of you already and, if not, such a report can be requested once you have a "release of information" from the parents. The report will probably not be as useful as it appears at first. Like most traditional assessments, there will be information like one-time scores on tests and grades. The assessment of academic level and "learning disabilities'' may be useful if that is an area in need of focus. What about report cards and grades? Unfortunately, although they are commonly available, they are of little use. Report cards come out too infrequently and grades like "A," "B," or "F" are very crude assessments of behavior long past. With younger children the report card may include grades or check marks on behaviors like "cooperates," "does homework," etc., but again it is a crude estimate months too late. "Units of credit," a certain number of which are necessary for graduation, are also available. Report cards and grades *are* important for school advancement, parents, juvenile courts, and college entrance so you may need to consider them and be alert as to how others use this information.

What kind of information from the school is likely to be of most interest to you as far as assessment of school behavior goes? Delinquent behaviors in the school may be of most importance. One bit of information easily obtained and quite reliable (except in some urban areas where it is too common and a relief to overloaded teachers!) is "truancy," or its reverse, attendance. It is the bottom line—is he or she attending school or not? It is easily measured because it is "yes" or "no," although "late" or "tardy" are more complex. Teachers, principals, or school psychologists are usually quite cooperative in giving you or the parents the information you request on a regular basis because it is their problem too, and if you can improve the problem behaviors in school it will make their work easier as well. You might wish to begin with a fairly general checklist of school behaviors like Fleischman and Conger's (1977) "Teacher's Daily Report Checklist" found in Table 4. It has three parts that pretty well cover the board: (a) behaviors that occur daily or are disruptive enough to result in removal from the classroom, (b) behaviors that seriously affect the child's academic performance, and (c) behaviors, perhaps of most interest here, that are delinquent or criminal.

Direct observation may be one alternative, either as an initial assessment or as a periodic assessment of progress. Cobb and Ray (in Patterson et al., 1975) have developed a standardized system for coding the following nineteen behaviors in the classroom: (a) gives approval, (b) complies, (c) appropriate talking with teacher, (d) appropriate interaction with peer, (e) volunteers in class, (f) interaction to teacher, (g) attending, (h) physical negative, (i) destructiveness, (j) gives disapproval, (k) noisy, (l) non-compliance, (m) unapproved play, (n) inappropriate talk with teacher, (o) inappropriate interaction with peer, (p) inappropriate locale (q)

Table 4

TEACHER'S DAILY REPORT CHECKLIST

Child's name: _____   Date: _____

School name: _____

School address: _____

Teacher's name: _____

School Specialist: _____

PART 1

DIRECTIONS: Put a checkmark next to each of the behaviors that are a serious problem because they either (1) occur almost daily, or (2) when they do occur, are so disruptive as to cause the child's being removed from the classroom or school.

```
Arguing with, defying teacher .............
Commanding, bossing peers ................
Competiveness, i.e., must be first ........
Damaging other children's property ........
Dawdling, being out of class too long .....
Disturbing, disrupting peers ..............
Excessive bathroom trips ..................
Fighting with peers .......................
Hitting, tripping, pushing, etc. ..........
Ignoring or disobeying teacher ............
Making a mess .............................
Out of seat ...............................
Running, roughhousing in classroom ........
Smoking ...................................
Tardy .....................................
Teasing, belittling peers .................
Yelling, calling out ......................
```

PART 2

DIRECTIONS: Put a checkmark next to each of the behaviors that seriously effect the child's academic performance.

```
Attending during instruction or
    explanation ...........................
Cheating ..................................
Finishing assignments .....................
Following directions ......................
Having homework ...........................
Participating .............................
Sloppiness ................................
Starting tasks when should ................
Staying on task ...........................
```

PART 3

Have any of the events listed below happened during the last two (2) months?

EVENTS

1. stealing   4. assaulting adults   7. other:
2. fire-setting   5. truancy   _____
3. vandalism   6. drugs, alcohol   _____

TABLE 4 (Continued)

```
For each event that occured, list (for each time the event
occured): the date it occured, who the repercussion was from, and
the location and value if the event was stealing, fire-setting,
or vandalism. If you can't remember the exact details, give your
best estimate.
```

```
                    WHO THE REPERCUSSION WAS FROM:

    1. none          3. school official     5. Other:

    2. parent or     4. police              6. Unknown:
       therapist                            _____


                    LOCATION

          1. school        2. community


                    VALUE

    1. negligible   4. $6 - $25           7. unknown:
    2. under $1     5. $26 - $200         _____
    3. $1 - $5      6. over $200
```

self-stimulation, (r) look around, and (s) not attending. Once particular problem behaviors in the school are determined, assessed, and deemed of particular relevance for changing delinquent behavior, you will need some on-going kind of assessment. This will necessitate some tactful negotiating with the school or teacher as it does require extra effort, although some school systems already have forms called "Daily Report Card." Alternatively, you can use a flexible daily assessment instrument like the Daily Behavior Card (Stumphauzer, 1974b) given in Figure 2. It can be filled out by the teacher, and takes only a few seconds a day; or it can be filled out by the youth (self-assessment) *and* countersigned by the teacher at the end of each week. The Daily Report Cards or Daily Behavior Cards can then be brought to you for each meeting as part of your on-going assessment of the program to change delinquent behavior and, in addition, are potentially of great interest to probation officers and juvenile courts.

8. ASSESSING AGGRESSION AND ASSERTION

Clearly, aggression is a major delinquent behavior. Not all aggression, of course, is a crime. For example, if a boy pushes his brother or if a girl slaps a boy's face we do not commonly think of these aggressions as crimes. If they were extreme or repetitive they might come before the court's attention, depending on the circumstances. By *aggression* we generally mean "the intentional harming of another person or property." Aggressive behaviors that are crimes for both adults and juveniles are such behaviors as murder, assault, and rape. With adolescents and children it is more likely that other lesser forms of aggression may also be considered delinquent behaviors: fighting, verbal hostility, vandalism and other destruction of property and belongings of others. Obviously, aggression may play an important role in the delinquent behavior to be changed and will, therefore, need to be assessed.

For the major criminal aggressive behaviors you may need to rely on the reports and records of police and probation. Direct observation is not likely. Report by others, teachers and parents or the youths themselves, is possible. The major criminal aggressive behaviors will likely be a matter for criminal investigation, and police and probation will be assessing them for court. The criminal definitions of these behaviors by the F.B.I. are given in Table 5.

Often, you will be involved in the assessment of aggressive delinquent behavior other than the major crimes: assault with a weapon, physical assault, fighting, verbal hostility, and destruction of property. Again, you can use the assessment approaches outlined earlier for other behaviors. Direct observation is possible, especially in the home and in the classroom. Simple measurement aids like the Daily Behavior Card can be used to record "number of fights" and so on. For a more complete assessment, you may want to draw up a three-part reporting form for parents, teacher, or for self-report with three columns following the Antecedents→Behavior→Consequents model (Table 6).

Is all aggression bad or undesirable? In a sense no, because in our general language we often use "aggressive" as a positive, desirable trait: "he is an aggressive salesman," for example. Recently, psychologists and others have differentiated between aggression and assertion. "*Aggression* is the intentional harm of another person while *assertion* is standing up for your own rights *without* hurting another person" (Stumphauzer, 1979, p. 195). Some delinquents are not assertive enough! You read that right. For many delinquents the most probable response is aggression. It is what they know best; perhaps their only response to frustration, the only way they know to get what they want. Other, socially inadequate delinquents, who may steal or do other solitary crimes, are neither aggressive or

Table 5

DEFINITIONS OF F.B.I. INDEX CRIMES

INDEX CRIMES	DEFINITIONS
Murder and nonnegligent manslaughter	Murder is defined as the willful killing of another. The classification of this offense, as well as other index crimes is based solely on police investigation as opposed to the determination of a court or other judicial body.
Aggravated assult	The unlawful attack by one person upon another for the purpose of inflicting severe bodily injury, usually accompanied by the use of a weapon or other means likely to produce death or serious bodily harm. Attempts are included, since it is not necessary that an injury result when a weapon is used which could result in serious injury if the crime were successfully completed.
Forcible rape	The carnal knowledge of a female through the use of force or threat of force. Assults to commit forcible rape are also included; statutory rape (without force) is not included.
Robbery	The stealing or taking of anything of value from the care, custody or control of a person in his presence, by force or threat of force. Assult to commit robbery and attempt at robbery are also included.
Burglary	The unlawfl entry of a structure to commit a felony or theft. The use of force to gain entry is not required to classify a crime as burglary.
Larceny-theft	The unlawful taking of property without the use of force, violence or fraud. Included are crimes such as shoplifting, pocket-picking and purse-snatching. Excluded are "con" games, forgery and the issuing of worthless checks.
Motor Vehicle Theft	The unlawful taking or stealing of a motor vehicle, including attempts. This definition excludes taking for temporary use by those persons having lawful access to the vehicle.

assertive. Both groups could benefit from programs called "assertion training." Shoemaker (1979) has reported such a program for delinquents using such attractive (for adolescents) methods as "Mental Kung Fu"—using your wits instead of your fists. This

Table 6

AN ABC BEHAVIOR EVALUATION

For each instance of an argument or a fight, as we have defined
them, record the following each day this week:

A	B	C
what was going on right before, what set it off?	describe the fight or argument, who did what?	what happended right after, what was the result?
1.	1.	1.
2.	2.	2.
3. etc.	3.	3.

approach will be covered in more detail later in Chapter Seven.
There are some assertion assessment tools that are available. The
Rathus Schedule for Assessing Assertive Behavior (1973) has been
utilized with adolescents and norms for comparison are given.
However, it is relatively complex and many adolescents have
difficulty reading it. Since aggression may be the undesirable
behavior and assertion the desirable or "instead" behavior, you
may want to assess both with a goal to changing deliquent behavior
in terms of decreasing aggression and increasing assertion.
The SASA (Stumphauzer Assertion Scale for Adolescents), which
assesses assertion, aggression, and nonassertiveness is found in
Table 7. Scoring of the SASA is achieved by totalling items 1–4 for
assertion, items 5–8 for aggression, and items 9–12 for nonassertiveness.

9. DSM III AND BEHAVIORAL ASSESSMENT

You may, depending on the structure and funding of your
program, need to work within the framework of the third edition of
the *Diagnostic and Statistical Manual of Mental Disorders* (DSM

III; American Psychiatric Association, 1980). Youths who are referred to you may already have DSM III diagnoses or your agency may be required to determine and clarify these diagnoses. The manual itself gives quite specific criteria, often in behavioral terms. Common primary diagnoses for delinquent youth are oppositional disorder, the various conduct disorders, substance abuse, etc. Criteria listed for each must be met.

Can DSM III be incorporated in behavioral assessment? In fact, DSM III relies much more on behavioral observation and behavioral criteria than DSM II. Powers (1984) has, in fact, developed a

Table 7
SASA
STUMPHAUZER ASSERTIVENESS SCALE
FOR ADOLESCENTS

Name _____   Date _____

INSTRUCTIONS: How much does each of the statements below describe you? Circle the number.	Not at all like me		In between		Very much like me
	1	2	3	4	5
1. In school I speak up when I have something to say.	1	2	3	4	5
2. If I was lost, I would ask a stranger for directions.	1	2	3	4	5
3. In a restaurant I tell the waitress if the food is not cooked right.	1	2	3	4	5
4. I would speak up if somebody cut in in line ahead of me.	1	2	3	4	5
5. I often lose my temper.	1	2	3	4	5
6. I am quick to get into fights.	1	2	3	4	5
7. I often argue.	1	2	3	4	5
8. I take what I want.	1	2	3	4	5
9. I am shy.	1	2	3	4	5
10. I avoid asking questions in class.	1	2	3	4	5
11. People take advantage of me.	1	2	3	4	5
12. I find it hard to say "no" to my friends.	1	2	3	4	5

AS_____   AG_____   NON_____

"syndromal diagnosis" approach which does link DSM III to the behavioral assessment approaches discussed here. He suggests an eight step model for the synthesis of DSM III and child behavioral assessment:

a. DSM III diagnosis,
b. determination of controlling variables,
c. examination of the relevant literature,
d. behavioral analysis of each DSM III criterion met,
e. formulate treatment hypotheses,
f. intervention,
g. evaluation,
h. follow-up.

10. BEHAVIORAL ASSESSMENT REPORT

We have covered a great many ways to meet the difficult task of assessing delinquent behavior. They vary with the particular delinquent behaviors presented, the family and social circumstances, and the resources available to you to complete your assessment. It is time to pull it all together in a social learning assessment report. It will summarize your findings, your conclusions about the learning and maintenence of the problems and assets, and form the basis for the plan to help delinquents change. In Table 8 you will find the outline for this purpose that I have been using in training therapists for the past twelve years. It was gleaned, in large part, from the classic work of Kanfer and Saslow (1969) on behavioral diagnosis. The report based on this outline can take the place of the usual "intake" or initial evaluation report.

While it will be obvious where the information already discussed will be summarized in the report, and how conclusions drawn, each section will be described briefly. The usual identification information is included in Part One. In Part Two, information on the referral is described. This is important from a social learning perspective because it may note *who* is motivated to change delinquent behavior. Since, as you have seen, the social learning environment controls and maintains delinquent behavior, Part Three includes a description of the environment of the youth. A description of the "interview behavior," a sample of behavior in the setting in which you will probably work, is given in section Four. Important

Table 8

BEHAVIORAL ASSESSMENT REPORT OUTLINE

1. IDENTIFICATION:
      name
      birthdate, age
      education
      occupation
      marital status
      physical description

2. REFERRAL:

Circumstances of the referral, who sought or motivated
the intervention?, presenting problem in client's own words,
frequency and circumstances of problem they report, what have
client or others done about the problem?

3. ENVIRONMENT:

Living circumstances, school or work circumstances, hours, family
members and important friends, how client spends spare time, get
a weekly schedule or diary.

4. INTERVIEW BEHAVIOR:

Behavior displayed in interview sessions, appropriateness of
social skills, reaction to social reinforcement of interviewer,
punctuality, motivation for change, etc.

5. ANALYSIS OF PROBLEM SITUATION:

      A. EXCESSIVE BEHAVIORS. Problem behaviors which occur
         1) too frequently, 2) too intensely, or 3) under
         inappropriate social circumstances.

      B. DEFICIENT BEHAVIOR. Classes of behaviors described
         as problematic because they do not occur
         1) with sufficient frequency, 2) in appropriate form,
         or 3) under socially desirable conditions.

      C. BEHAVIOR ASSETS. Nonproblematic, desirable behaviors
         which the client does display. What he or she does
         well, special abilities, what they are proud of.

6. CLARIFICATION OF PROBLEM SITUATIONS:

For each of the excessive and deficient behaviors noted, who
objects to these behaviors and who tends to support them
(attention for them, etc.)? What consequences or results (both
immediate and long-range) do each of these behaviors have for the
client and for significant others? What new problems in
living would successful therapy pose for the client? Under what
exact conditions do the problems behaviors occur? Do others agree
with the client's description of his problem behavior? Does the
client have have biological limitations?

7. REINFORCEMENT SURVEY

What does the client rank as incentives in the order of their
importance to him or her (as effective in initiating or
maintaining their behavior)? (see "Favorite Things Survey") What
has been the client's experience with these reinforcers? Which
people have the most control over the client's current behaviors?
What are the major aversive stimuli for this client? What
relationships, activities, or objects would the client like more
of? Who would he or she like to spend more time with? Doing what?

TABLE 8 (Continued)

8. ANALYSIS OF SELF-CONTROL:

In what particular situations can the client control the problem behaviors? Is this control gained by manipulation of self or others? What stimuli, conditions, persons, or reinforcers tend to change his or her self-controlling behavior? To what extent can the client's self-control be used or expanded in the intervention program?

9. ANALYSIS OF THE SOCIAL-CULTURAL ENVIRONMENT:

Who are the most important people in the client's environment and how can they influence the client in changing? What are the norms in the client's milieu for these problem behaviors? Is there support in his or her immediate environment for the changes in behavior that are being sought? Are there forces (e.g., peers) which may exert antitherapeutic influences? Is there a change in the environment anticipated?

10. BASELINES:

In may be desirable to determine the frequency and stability of behaviors before any intervention (baseline or baserate). These can be determined from records (school, etc.), direct observation, self-recording, or record keeping by significant others (parents, etc.). Baselines are important both a) as initial assessments of the level or frequency of the problem behaviors, and b) for comparison to levels of these behaviors after intervention in order to evaluate effectiveness and to adjust treatment.

11. TREATMENT PLAN:

Based on the above analysis of behavior, what are the logical step for intervention? What are reasonable short-term goals, and how could they be achieved using data from this analysis? What are the long-range goals and how will the behavior therapy outlined here gradually reach those goals? Who will be involved directly in the behavior change program and is there informed consent? Stress generalization to natural controls in this treatment plan, either in terms of environmental change or in terms of self-control. State treatment plan or suggestions in a way that others will be able to utilize if the case is transferred, or if the behavior change program is carried out elsewhere.

behaviors, both positive and negative, are classified into three categories in section Five: excessive, deficient, and asset. Behaviorally descriptive terms like "fighting in school" are used rather than generalities such as "aggressive." Asset behaviors, like "plays football well" are stressed because an attempt may be made to increase their frequency in place of delinquent behaviors. Under section Six each key behavior is further clarified with conclusions from your social learning assessment about what is maintaining the delinquent behaviors and, perhaps, what is *not* reinforcing the "good," incompatible, nondelinquent, asset behaviors. Other important points are made as well. In Part Seven the results of your reinforcement assessment are summarized. Part Eight describes your assessment of this youth's self-control. Noteworthy is Kanfer and Saslow's (1969) conceptualization of self-control. For our purposes here, under exactly what circumstance do the delinquent behaviors *not* occur? Can those circumstances of self-control be expanded? Part Ten can be a verbal summary of the baserate or baseline of the key behaviors in your assessment, the rate of these behaviors *before* any intervention (a necessity to evaluate the progress in changing delinquent behavior). Included with your report can be the actual forms or graphs used to assess baselines of behavior. Based directly on the assessment you have accomplished, and your social learning analysis above, what are the logical choices and steps for changing delinquent behavior: the social learning intervention plan (Part Eleven)? These can be selected from the many approaches described in later parts of this work, or some combination thereof. It will become more clear which treatment strategies fit which problems as you review the remaining chapters. This decision can be reached after a discussion of your findings with the youth, the family, and other key persons (teacher, probation officer). At the same time, short and long range goals can be set, keeping in mind that learning, including these social learning programs, is gradual. Some behaviors, like firesetting, require immediate attention and may take precedent at first over "bad attitude." It will necessarily depend in part on the motivation of those involved, the resources available, and the availability of the particular methods of changing delinquent behavior. To further clarify the assessment process by way of example, a sample behavioral assessment report is given in Table 9.

Table 9

SAMPLE BEHAVIORAL ASSESSMENT REPORT

Identification

Victor S., a 15 year old male (birthdate 8-15-80) who attends regular 9th grade classes at Roosevelt High School. Usually dressed in T-shirt and jeans, he is slightly less than average in height and

TABLE 9 (Continued)

weight. There is a tattoo on his right hand (''Loco''), which he says was done in juvenile hall two years ago.

Referral

Referred to this clinic by Probation Department following arrest for stealing $10.00 on school grounds. Probation report also notes problems of truancy, arrest at age 13 for theft of money ($20.00) from locker at school, and unspecified ''family problems.'' Victor and his mother have been told ''this is your last chance.''

Environment

Victor lives with his mother, two older brothers (age 16 and 19), a younger sister (12), and a younger brother (11) in a two bedroom apartment in an ethnically mixed, lower income section of southeast Los Angeles. Victor's father left the family ten years ago and, in Victor's words, ''he has a new family.'' Victor knows where his father lives and currently sees him ''about four times a year.'' There is a juvenile gang in his neighborhood, but Victor denies membership, ''but I know the guys because I grew up with them.''

Interview Behavior

Victor sat up straight and had increased eye-contact when talking about cars, baseball, and his brother Ted. He sank in his chair and looked away, tapping his foot, when his mother described his problems. He appeared very responsive to the interviewer's attention and praise; he looked directly at him and continued speaking on the topic. Victor and his mother were observed in a structured situation: they were asked to discuss ''curfew hours'' for 10 minutes while the interviewer observed from the next room. Mrs. S. attempted to set a rule of ''be home by 10:00 PM,'' but he protested and she gave up at which point he smiled broadly and then she smiled as well, throwing her hands up. Mother appears not to pay attention when Victor talks about his interest in cars, jobs, and baseball. Victor appeared socially skilled at speaking up for himself, in conversation skills, eye-contact, and in controlling his mother. He admits stealing money 10 to 12 times at school (''because I needed it'') and shoplifting ''small things and clothes'' since age 10.

TABLE 9 (Continued)

Analysis of Problem Situation

A. Excessive Behavior

1. theft of money 10–12 times at school (.50 to $20.00)
2. shoplifting (clothing and sports items, .25 to $20.00)

B. Deficient Behavior

1. school attendance (truant 20% of last semester)
2. employment (unemployed)

C. Behavior Assets

1. social/conversation skills
2. skilled in baseball
3. auto mechanics

Clarification of Problem Situation

Victor's excessive behaviors (theft of money, clothing and sporting goods) are objected to by the school and shopowners. These behaviors appear to be stimulated by opportunity (sight and availability of items), by not having "enough" spending money, and maintained by (1) ease of thefts (success), (2) having the desired objects immediately, (3) by self-praise, and (4) by attention from mother in the form of increased time and "concern."

With regard to deficient behaviors, truancy is stimulated by friends who are also "cutting school" to "do something better," and/or tests or other scheduled events he would like to avoid. The immediate consequences of truancy are positive ("fun," etc.) and later there may or may not be mild negative consequences (telephone call to mother). Although Victor has worked in the past (newspaper route, gardening), he has not worked for two years, saying "there are no jobs, there's no time." Unemployment is maintained further by his mother who not only agrees with his belief in job unavailability, but who also gives him money noncontingently "when he needs it."

Victor is a skilled, likable young man with many behavior assets. Friends and strangers quickly stimulate his conversation skills and join-in and otherwise give him attention to maintain this skill. He says "I have a way with people." Baseball, over the past five years

TABLE 9 (Continued)

has been stimulated by his big brother Ted, by Summer, and the proximity to the park a block from his home. He has been reinforced for the skill by success and attention plus, he says, "it feels good to get out there." Finally, he says he's always been interested in cars and auto mechanics. He says, with some self-reinforcing praise that "I can tear down and rebuild an engine." These skills were stimulated by his brother Ted who works on his car at home and by the auto mechanics class at school.

Reinforcement Survey

Through use of the Favorite Things survey and interview it was determined that Victor ranked the following as his strongest reinforcers (beginning with the strongest): (1) attention/praise from brother Ted, (2) attention/praise from mother, (3) money, (4) access to a car, (5) opportunity to play baseball, and (6) new clothing. He noted that the punishments he dislikes the most are (1) being locked up in juvenile hall and (2) being ignored. He was responsive to the interviewer's attention and praise (stayed on topic or increased verbalizations). Victor does utilize self-reinforcement (self-statements of pride and accomplishment such as "I'm good at . . .") as well as self-punishment ("That was stupid"). He would like to spend more time with brother Ted, his father, working on cars, and playing sports. His mother makes some of his favorite foods which he considers "treats" (spaghetti, tacos, ribs, and German chocolate cake—preferably in the same meal!).

Analysis of Self-Control

Victor steals, but he does *not* steal at home or from friends. Thus he demonstrates self-control over stealing in those circumstances. He also reports that he does not steal when he has money. He only steals alone, and not in the presence of people he knows. In fact, he reported stopping a theft when he saw a friend approaching in a store. Thus, the presence of relatives or friends might be used to increase environmental control as self-control is further developed. To the contrary, he usually is not truant on his own, but usually when friends also cut school. Although he lives in a "gang territory," Victor has not joined the gang and he reportedly interacts with members "with no problem."

TABLE 9 (Continued)

Analysis of Social-Cultural Environment

No change in Victor's environment is planned. However, he will probably be placed in a probation "camp" if he is arrested again. He lives in a crowded household in which there are strong family ties and affection. His mother is caring but ineffective, often giving attention for problem behavior. The other most important person is his 19 year old brother Ted, who works but reportedly does like and spend time with Victor. He might be an important agent of change in treatment as a model and reinforcer. The neighborhood is a "tough" one, but this does not appear to play a direct role in Victor's problem behaviors. The family has lived here for 16 years and have a strong sense of community: "we wouldn't move if we could."

Diagnosis (DSM III)

Axis I:	312.21 Conduct Disorder, Socialized, Nonaggressive
Axis II:	none
Axis III:	"asthma"
Axis IV:	4: moderate stressors
Axis V:	4: fair adaptive functioning

Prognosis

Fair to good with treatment.

Baselines

Victor admits stealing "10 to 12 times" at school in the last two years (an average of once every 2 months) and shoplifting small items "about once a month" and large items "only twice." He says he has not done either theft since last arrest, and there is no evidence to the contrary. School reports a baseline of 80% attendance last semester. He has not been employed for two years. Social/conversation skills are at a very high (undetermined at this point) rate. Victor reports playing baseball "about twice a week." He works on auto mechanics "once or twice a week" at home with Ted and three times a week at school. Victor has agreed, in exchange for $3.00 allowance a week, to begin self-assessing the following behaviors

TABLE 9 (Continued)

on a Daily Behavior Card: (1) worked on car, (2) played baseball, (3) number of times I steal, and (4) attended school.

Treatment Plan

The treatment plan is a combination of family contracting, social skills group, and self-control training. A contract is planned between Victor, his family (mother and brother Ted), the probation officer, and the therapist beginning with the general agreement "In order to keep Victor out of trouble . . . we agree to work together." (See Chapter Six.) Victor, his mother, and the therapist signed this first agreement. They are taking a copy for Ted to sign and will then take it to a probation meeting next week and agree to bring the completed copy to our next session. One of the first points in the next contract will be that "In order to do one thing leading to getting off probation . . . Victor agrees to attend Dr. Stumphauzer's Social Skills group for 10 sessions." While Victor is socially skilled in many areas (indeed, he can model these skills for others), he is unemployed and money is central to problem behaviors. Three of the ten sessions deal with getting and keeping jobs. Also, he would benefit from the session on problem solving and on how to say "no" to peer pressure to be truant. Other steps in the contracts should deal with (1) shifting mother's attention from problem behaviors to attending school, getting a job, and compliance with this program, (2) gaining Ted's cooperation in modeling employment and utilizing his social attention for Victor's behavior improvements, and (3) spelling out exact negative consequences for probation violation, especially the very real impending "lock up" for another arrest, and detailing exactly what will be required to get off probation.

Self-control training should focus on undermining any belief that it is "ok" to steal, and on self-measuring/self-assessing behaviors incompatible with problem behaviors (*earning* money, *attending* school), and self-reinforcement. Assessment of these behaviors, and any crimes, will be maintained. Employment in a service station or garage (perhaps beginning with "cleaning up" and then "helping") seems one reasonable goal. Identification with Ted and employers will be encouraged. Treatment is anticipated to be once weekly (combination of family contracting, and individual self-control training) as well as 10 sessions in the social skills group. Contact/-cooperation will be maintained with the school and probation

TABLE 9 (Continued)

officer. The treatment goal is to gradually shift this social learning program to the improved natural control of the family (mother and Ted) and to Victor himself whose asset behaviors and self-control can be expanded to not only "stay out of trouble" but to lead a more rewarding life.

As noted earlier, behavioral evaluation is an ongoing process. Those assessments utilized here should be refined and continued throughout counseling and during a reasonable "follow-up" period. The treatment plan or particular approach must remain flexible and vary with any need for change based on the continuing assessment and new circumstances that arise. Behavior assessment then, is the first and one of the most crucial steps in helping delinquents change.

SUMMARY

This chapter reviewed the rationale and concepts involved in the behavioral evaluation of delinquents and provided several approaches and instruments for organizing information about youths in trouble. The function of behavioral assessment is to gather and organize information with a goal of utility in helping delinquents change and in measuring this change.

Usually the first one or two counseling or therapy sessions are used to complete an initial behavioral assessment: interviews, direct observation, development of specialized measurements, and formulation and synthesis of a social learning analysis, intervention plan, and method of on-going assessment of behavior. The application of several instruments was reviewed: parent evaluation form, reinforcement survey, a daily behavior card, and teacher's daily checklist. Others are found elsewhere in the book. A synthesis of DSM III and behavioral assessment was noted.

Finally, the format and process for preparing a behavioral assessment report were presented and a sample report was provided. In it the information gathered is specified, preliminary conclusions about social learning variables are drawn, baseline measures are noted, and an intervention or treatment plan logically following from the behavioral analysis is formulated. This process and report are offered as an alternative to traditional interviewing and evaluation reports.

On a larger scale, behavioral assessment can be expanded for use in planning and evaluation of programs in schools, institutions, and in the community as noted in subsequent chapters. The next chapter reviews four social learning principles basic to the remaining chapters of the book. The application of each in understanding the development of delinquent behavior and in helping delinquents change is discussed.

READINGS

1. Kanfer, F. H., & Saslow, G. (1969). Behavioral diagnosis. In C. M. Franks (Ed.) *Behavior therapy: Appraisal and status.* New York: McGraw-Hill.

2. Ollendick, T. H., & Hersen, M. (Eds.) (1984). *Child behavioral assessment: Principles and procedures.* New York: Pergamon Press.

3. Mash, E. J., & Terdal, L. G. (Eds.) (1981). *Behavioral assessment of childhood disorders.* New York: Guilford.

CHAPTER 4

Social Learning Principles: Learning and Unlearning Delinquent Behavior

Knowledge of the principles of social learning is basic to understanding both how delinquent behavior develops (is learned) and how it can be changed (unlearned). This will help considerably in unraveling any mystery about how children become delinquent, why other children do not, and why some treatments work better than others. Since delinquent behavior *is* learned, it is paramount to determine how that learning takes place if one is to understand delinquent behavior and what can be done to change, or even better, to prevent it.

In this chapter four basic social learning principles are given and are followed with two sets of examples. These principles are quoted from *Behavior Modification Principles* (Stumphauzer, 1977), a programmed introduction and training manual on twenty-two such principles and it should be consulted for more thorough coverage. In the first set of examples, illustrations of how that particular principle can play a role in *learning delinquent behavior* are given. In the second set of examples, illustrations of how that same principle might or has been used in modifying or *helping delinquent behavior change*. While these four basic principles are stressed, other related principles are discussed as well. These principles are building blocks utilized in the remainder of the book and will be referred to in subsequent chapters. The application of each will be noted repeatedly in subsequent chapters. The first two principles (positive reinforcement and modeling) deal with *increasing* behavior or making it more frequent. The remaining two principles (extinction and punishment) deal with *decreasing* behavior or making it less likely. The reader should note that *both* types of principles are active in teaching delinquent behavior as well as teaching nondelinquent or productive behavior.

1. PRINCIPLE OF POSITIVE REINFORCEMENT

IF A CONSEQUENCE OR RESULT OF A BEHAVIOR HAS THE EFFECT OF *INCREASING* THE STRENGTH OR FREQUENCY OF THAT BEHAVIOR, THEN *POSITIVE REINFORCEMENT* HAS TAKEN PLACE.

A. *Learning Delinquent Behavior*

Positive reinforcement, more popularly called "reward," is probably *the* most basic learning principle. It is constantly at work in practically all the behavior we acquire whether it is learning to talk, to drive an automobile, learning how to counsel and help others, or learning to rob and steal. Let us focus on children learning to steal—perhaps the most common delinquent behavior. If a young child takes a toy from a store and there is no immediate negative consequence (he does not get caught and punished), then he has experienced a number of things. First, he discovered a quick and easy way to get something he wants—just take it. The reinforcement or reward was *immediate,* which is the most effective timing for learning new behavior. He learned that if he is a little careful he won't get caught and there isn't much chance of punishment. Finally, he learned (just by experimenting this first time) a particular *technique* of stealing that was reinforced. There was a whole chain of behaviors: seeing the toy, thinking about taking it, waiting for the clerk and customers to walk away, taking the toy, hiding it, leaving the store, playing with the toy, and perhaps even saying things to himself like "well that was easy, I'm pretty smart and I got what I wanted. They can't catch me!" All of this chain was positively reinforced. It is now more probable or more likely that he will steal again the next time he wants something that he can't get as easily any other way. His stealing behavior will gradually change or be *shaped* by successive approximation depending on what variations of stealing work the best (get rewarded): which stores to choose, how to distract the clerk, how to pick up and conceal the goods, and so on. *Social reinforcement,* positive reinforcement in the form of attention and praise, will most likely become part of the picture as well. He may share his experience (and reward!) with a friend who might have "new respect" for him because of his stealing or because of the great new toys he has stolen. Even being caught often leads to social reinforcement and not to punishment as is commonly believed. It is not unusual for a child to receive *more* (not less) attention from parents, teachers, and peers when they get in trouble.

Stumphauzer (1976b) reported a case that illustrates these very points—a twelve year old girl who stole "uncontrollably" was described. Through a behavior analysis, or study of the behavior and what controlled it, much of the mystery of her "uncontrollable" stealing disappeared. Often the girl was not caught; positive reinforcement (getting what she wanted) was quite regular over at least a five year period. In addition the girl was attending a Catholic school and when she was caught she was sent to the principal, a favorite of hers, and they prayed together for a cure from her "illness!" Good grief! Finally, she would be sent home from school (an all-too-common reinforcement!) where her parents would add further social attention and concern. Stealing was heavily and routinely reinforced.

The learning of delinquent behavior does not stop when a youth is sent to a juvenile hall residential youth center. Indeed, institutions for delinquents may well be a place where further delinquent behavior is reinforced and shaped. A school for delinquents may indeed fit that title only too well: a school for learning delinquent behavior. For example, in a series of studies of institutions for girls it was found that the girls regularly reinforced antisocial or delinquent behavior in their peers while the institutional staff were much less consistent (Buehler, Patterson & Furniss, 1966).

In summary, positive reinforcement is the major "teacher" of virtually all delinquent behavior. The specifics of this reinforcement (type of reinforcement, the timing, and who is doing the reinforcing) must be discovered by behavioral analysis (Chapter Three). Only then can a youth counselor, teacher, probation officer, or parent hope to change the behavior.

B. Helping Delinquents Change

The principle of positive reinforcement is just as important in modifying or changing delinquent behavior as it is in establishing the behavior in the first place. It is both highly effective *and* ethical—it utilizes a positive stimulus (a reward) and does not inflict pain or harm as some forms of punishment do. There are two basic strategies that utilize positive reinforcement in helping delinquents change and both have been widely used: (a) reinforcing instances or time periods in which the delinquent behavior does *not* occur, and (b) reinforcing behavior that is in itself incompatible with the delinquent behavior. Both rely on positive reinforcement.

Let us return to the case of stealing. After establishing what is reinforcing for the particular youth (see Chapter Three), reinforcement is given for *not* stealing. In the case mentioned earlier the twelve year old girl agreed to earn ten cents for ice cream (before inflation!) for each day she did not steal. In addition, her parents switched from giving so much attention for stealing episodes to giving special attention and praise for days and weeks of *not* stealing. This application of positive reinforcement within family contracting (see Chapter Eight), combined with *self-reinforcement* in which the girl was trained to praise herself for the new-found self-control ("I'm proud that I didn't steal today, I *can* do it!"), resulted in a rapid cessation in stealing lasting through the one and one half years of follow-up. Similar applications of positive reinforcement have been made for *not* taking drugs and for *not* fighting.

In other instances, with other kinds of delinquent behaviors, one is usually much further ahead if one can reinforce behavior that is *incompatible* with the delinquent behavior. By incompatible we mean a behavior that does not "go with," or is often opposite to, the delinquent behavior. If one occurs, the other cannot. So the goal is first to determine if the delinquent behavior has an incompatible opposite or counterpart and then to reinforce *it*. As that behavior becomes more frequent or probable through reinforcement, the delinquent behavior will become less frequent.

One simple example is truancy from school; certainly a common problem. Again, effective and strong reinforcers are determined and then consistently applied for the incompatible or opposite behavior—*attending* school. A gradual shaping program may be needed—first reinforce a partial day, then whole days and finally weeks of attendance. Positive reinforcement has been the cornerstone of the highly acclaimed Achievement Place style of home for problem youths (see Chapter Twelve on group homes). School *attendance* (not truancy) and school *achievement* (not failure) are positively reinforced with points which can be traded in for desirable activities and goods.

Youth unemployment is often part of the complex picture of youth crime. How is one to alter it? Many youths and adults are paid (that is, reinforced) for *not* working. This is no answer and may even be part of the problem. Providing more jobs would certainly help in areas of high youth unemployment. Simply reinforcing having a job, although it is incompatible with unemployment, may not be enough. As some researchers have found, it may be necessary to break down the complex behavior "having a job" into steps or *job skills* such as applying for a job, relating to supervisors, being on time, handling job problems, etc. (see Chapter Eleven). Through behavioral assessment it may be determined that a particular unemployed youth may be lacking in one or all of these pro-employment behaviors. Those skills can be shaped and acquired with a positive reinforcement program as demonstrated by Mills and Walter (1979). The "natural" positive reinforcements that keep many of us working (wages, praise, accomplishment, social identity) may be too delayed for youth new to the work-force, and more immediate praise and tangible reinforcements may be necessary that first day (that first minute?) on the job until regular employment can be gradually shaped. Once maintained it will be a key set of behaviors that will be incompatible with delinquency.

2. PRINCIPLE OF MODELING AND IMITATION

BEHAVIOR MAY BE LEARNED OR MODIFIED SIMPLY AS A FUNCTION OF *OBSERVING* THE BEHAVIOR OF A MODEL, AND BY *OBSERVING* THE CONSEQUENCES OF THE MODEL'S BEHAVIOR.

A. *Learning Delinquent Behavior*

A great deal of what we all learn is by observing or watching someone else do something first, and then try doing it ourselves. This social learning process is called modeling (displaying the behavior) and imitation (copying the behavior). It is especially effective for complex behaviors. For example, in learning to drive an automobile it would take forever if we just relied on positive reinforcement and a gradual shaping of the behavior. Instead, we watch our instructor (model) closely and then try to match what they did behind the wheel (we imitate). Learning to be a therapist or counselor is no different. We don't usually rely on trial and error learning (sometimes we do!), but often we watch a supervisor or someone else interview and counsel, or read about experts, or listen to tapes, and then learn from them. Positive reinforcement comes into play *after* we imitate—if we drive the car well, if we match the behavior of supervisors, and if therapy strategies "work" for us.

Much of delinquent behavior is learned by modeling and imitation. We hear popular references to this such as "he hangs around with the wrong crowd, they're a bad influence." There is no question that a great deal of delinquent behavior is learned by imitating powerful peer-models. It is important to understand how this process works if one is to help change it.

Do children learn violence by watching it on television and in movies? There is much evidence that they do. In a classic study by Bandura, Ross, and Ross (1963) it was demonstrated that some novel forms of aggression toward a inflated "Bobo" doll were indeed taught both by live and filmed models displaying the same type of aggression. In our studies of gang violence in Los Angeles we found modeling and imitation a key to understanding the development of this "gang behavior" (Stumphauzer, Aiken & Veloz, 1977). In some instances a young gang member (imitator) was even named after an older gang member that they emulated (model): "Sneaky" and "Little Sneaky." Similarly, modeling and imitation play an important role in drug abuse. In a study of adolescents learning to drink, for example, Stumphauzer (1980) found that youths imitated both the drinking behavior of their peers and their parents.

In looking at a particular delinquent it is important, in the behavioral assessment, to determine who his or her particular models are and exactly how they exert their influence on the delinquent's behavior—especially if this influence is continuing. How do they model for and reinforce this particular youth? At the same time it is important to discover if models are potentially available to display incompatible, nondelinquent behavior (nondelinquent friends, for example). The key influence of nondelinquent peers was described in Chapter Two.

B. Helping Delinquents Change

The principle of modeling and imitation can play an influential part in helping delinquents change as well. It may sound incredible, but many delinquents don't know how to do any behaviors other than their delinquent behaviors. These are very real deficits. They have to learn these new behaviors and modeling and imitation, followed by reinforcement, is probably the most effective means.

Let us return to the specific case of aggression. Aggressive delinquents may not really know any other way to react to even minimal stress and provocations. Their first choice (the most probable behavior) is the one they have learned so well, the one that up until now has "worked" (been reinforced) for them. In the short run if they strike out, hit, curse, or somehow harm the other person, they often get what they want—at least for the moment. Remember, as noted earlier, immediate or "for the moment" reinforcement is the most influential. Assertion training or social skills training (see Chapter Seven) may be of use. Train delinquents to be *more* assertive? Surly assertive delinquents are the last thing we need! We differentiate assertion from aggression: assertion is standing up for your legitimate rights *without taking away the rights of others,* while aggression is inflicting harm or pain on others. Social skills like assertion can be taught with modeling and imitation. Shoemaker (1979), for example, has developed such a program for institutionalized delinquents. Both the group leader and other youths model assertive and nonaggressive ways to handle normally provacative situations (e.g., "another guy calls you a name") with some creative session formats like "Mental Kung Fu" which includes Stand Tall, Think Smart, and Be Self-Controlled. Once the boys did imitate this newly learned assertion they received positive reinforcement.

Two other studies further underscore the potential uses of modeling and imitation in modifying delinquent behavior. Stumphauzer (1972) utilized prestigious, older inmates in a federal youth prison as models to increase the delay of gratification of younger, newly admitted imates. Observation of the models making delay choices ("I can wait for that, I'd rather have two magazines in a week instead of one now") greatly changed the subsequent choices of the observers—they changed and imitated the delaying behavior or waiting for more valuable things in the future.

In a study of adolescents who were learning *not* to drink, Stumphauzer (1983) found that there was often a nondrinking model who greatly influenced the youth ("I don't need to drink or use drugs." "I get high on life.") In summary, modeling and imitation are vitally important modes of learning—especially in adolescents—and play a key role in teaching delinquent behavior as well as in learning incompatible, nondelinquent, prosocial behavior.

3. PRINCIPLE OF EXTINCTION

WHEN BEHAVIOR IS NO LONGER FOLLOWED BY REIN-FORCEMENT, THE BEHAVIOR WILL *DECREASE* IN STRENGTH OR FREQUENCY AND WILL GRADUALLY *EX-TINGUISH*.

A. Learning Delinquent Behavior

Extinction is the first of two learning principles (extinction and punishment) that *decrease* behavior or make behavior less probable. What part does extinction play in learning or acquiring delinquent behavior? As you are aware, the youths we call delinquent don't only do criminal behaviors, but also, at times, act in positive, good, or noncriminal ways. Gradually, as a child develops if these *non*delinquent behaviors are tried and *do not* meet with positive reinforcement they will extinguish—they will happen less often, will become less likely. At the same time that these "good" behaviors are being extinguished or dropping out, delinquent behaviors are being increased by modeling and/or reinforcement. The combined result is the learning or development of delinquent or criminal behaviors. These behaviors "work;" they get results (and quickly!). The nondelinquent behaviors didn't "work," there was no payoff and, for the most part, they extinguished. There may still be an occasional attempt at nondelinquent behaviors, but they won't continue if they don't meet with positive reinforcement (praise, attention, desired objects, or even self-satisfaction).

Perhaps some examples will make this process more clear. A young child finds money and turns it in. She gets no reaction, no thank you, nothing. She is, therefore, less likely to turn in "lost" money again. A boy is faced with a choice: another boy in his school has a "hot wheels" toy car that he wants very much for himself; it crosses his mind that he could take it or he could try some other way to get one. He goes home, asks his mother if there is some way he can earn the two dollars needed to buy one. If this nondelinquent, "good" behavior of "earning the things you want" is not reinforced (in a number of such circumstances) it will extinguish. The next day he steals the car. He has it immediately. No hassle. Now, in addition, he may have to lie about how he got the car ("I earned it in school; honest."). The next time he wants something, what is the probability of trying to earn it and the likelihood of stealing it? Those probabilities have changed. We have observed the beginning of the learning of delinquency as it was being shaped by the dual principles of extinction and positive reinforcement. But how can extinction be utilized to change already existent delinquent behavior?

B. Helping Delinquents Change

When behavior is no longer reinforced it will gradually extinguish or happen less often. This is also the case with delinquent behavior, but it is not as simple as it sounds. There are two necessary requisites. First of all you will need to discover what the rewards or reinforcements for the delinquent behavior are. The behavioral analysis discussed in Chapter Three will help a great deal in this regard. Often, the reinforcements are the consequents *immediately* following the behavior such as attention from peers (e.g., for fighting) and obtaining objects (e.g., by stealing) that they could not easily obtain in other ways. The second requisite is more of a problem, and it is the implication that once you discover what the rewards are for the delinquent behavior, that you (or someone you can influence) (a) has control of the reinforcements and (b) is willing to stop them. With adolescents many of the reinforcements come from outside the influence of the home and the counseling situation. Peers exert a great deal of reinforcement and, unfortunately, often in ways we cannot observe or change. Indeed, a delinquent peer group may be quite vested in continuing the reinforcement for delinquent behavior. There are instances, however, when delinquent behavior is maintained by reinforcers in the family (attention, for example). This seems to be true especially in families in which the children only gain attention for "bad" behavior like fighting, school problems, being arrested, etc. Some attention, even being yelled at or "guilt tripped," is better than no attention.

In order to change delinquent behaviors utilizing extinction one must arrange for the reinforcements to cease. The family or teacher might be convinced to do this, but extinction (by itself) is a slow and torturous process—for the parent or teacher! The behavior might *increase* temporarily and then gradually become less frequent. This process is often punishing to all those near the adolescent. For example, fighting and arguring might temporarily increase. Also, many delinquent, criminal behaviors must cease immediately and not occur again, and one cannot wait for extinction to occur. Firesetting, for example, must stop *now*. Fortunately, there is a way out of this dilemma. That is to *shift* the reinforcers that were reinforcing the delinquent, problem behaviors to good, desirable behaviors so that these behaviors will increase. For example, if truancy was reinforced with getting attention from the boy's father, the attention given for truancy should cease (extinction) and instead attention should be given by the father for *attending* school (positive reinforcement). This is a good example of using a combination of social learning principles to change delinquent behavior. If a child shoplifts to get the things he or she wants, then the articles should be taken away (extinction) *and* a way should be found so that these objects could be earned by working (positive reinforcement). In any case, the counselor or therapist themselves are not likely to have control over the reinforcers for delinquent behavior, so they must discover who does (parent, teacher, friend, or the youths themselves) and influence them to cease or shift to other, positive behavior.

4. PRINCIPLE OF PUNISHMENT

IF THE *PRESENTATION* OF AN *AVERSIVE* STIMULUS AS THE CONSEQUENCE OF A BEHAVIOR *DECREASES* THE STRENGTH OR FREQUENCY OF THAT BEHAVIOR, THEN PUNISHMENT HAS TAKEN PLACE.

A. Learning Delinquent Behavior

Does punishment play a role in the development of delinquent behavior? It does indeed. It has been found, for example, that punishment is the most common child rearing principle used by parents of delinquents (Stuart, 1970). As young children, delinquents are exposed to more punishment than nondelinquents. In fact one could make a case for excessive parental punishment as one of the major causes of delinquency. Patterson (1982) has described the common coercive family process of the youth acting in a way counter to the wishes of parents who react punitively and then the youth in turn reacts aggressively.

What do children learn from parents who punish them so often? For one thing they learn (through modeling and imitation) how to punish others. Their models (parents) show them that the way to control others is to be aggressive and to hurt people when they don't do what you want. This is probably why there is so much support for the belief that children who are abused grow up to be child abusers themselves. When parents rely exclusively on punishment, their children learn a series of "what *not* to do" but they only learn "what *to* do" by trial and error. Also, there is evidence to suggest that those who punish are generally avoided. This might form part of an explanation of teenagers avoiding parents (who punish) while seeking time with the peer group (which utilizes positive reinforcement). Finally, there is the general punisher called incarceration (jail, juvenile hall, youth camp, etc.). As already pointed out, Buehler, Patterson, and Furniss (1966) found that a great deal of delinquent behavior is learned while being "punished" by incarceration with other delinquents.

B. Helping Delinquents Change

Punishment is the *most popular* principle for changing delinquent behavior. Punishment is the *least effective* principle for changing delinquent behavior. In fact, I bet many readers will turn to this section to find "bigger and better" punishments for delinquents. Does punishment change delinquent behavior? Yes and no. By definition it does. That is, if the consequence decreases the behavior it follows, then it is a punisher. But how about all those consequences that are commonly called "punishment" like arrest, jail, being yelled at by a teacher, and being beaten by a parent? Well, as a matter of fact, they often *do not* decrease the behavior and, therefore, are not punishment according to the psychological definition given above. In fact, some of them might actually act to *increase* the behavior and would be—believe it or not—positive reinforcement! That's right, a slap or a yell could function as positive reinforcement. Our behavioral analysis of juvenile gangs found that arrest and short-term incarceration often functioned as a reward (Stumphauzer, Aiken, & Veloz, 1977). Yet, these supposed "punishments" are the most popularly applied method for changing delinquent behavior. Many suggest we need to "get tough" and use them even more often! Even punishments that do stop behavior may only "suppress" it for a short time and the behavior will occur again later. This temporary suppression may be, however, one clue to the popularity of punishment. If a parent, teacher, or guard in an institution uses a punisher and it even temporarily stops the behavior, then *they* are reinforced for using it and are likely to apply it again. Also, the physical aspects of striking out or hurting the source of frustration (the child) may be reinforcing, even if it doesn't work in the long run. In addition, there are the myriad of ethical and legal problems in using punishment. If there was an effective punishment, say a strong electric shock, it could not be used on ethical/legal grounds.

Can punishment play any role in changing delinquent behavior? Possibly. The behavior may need to be stopped *immediately,* and punishment might be used to get the behavior to stop *and then* positive reinforcement can be utilized to shape other behavior. Two forms of punishment with less ethical/legal problems than inflicting pain are time-out and response cost (Stumphauzer, 1977). In time-out, the reinforcement is withheld following undesirable behavior *but* only for one to five minutes. Tyler (1967) withheld pool-playing for a few moments for those delinquents who misbehaved while shooting pool in an institutional setting. In response cost, delinquent behaviors would result in a loss of reinforcers or in a cost of some kind. This is especially useful in a token economy or point earning program. Tokens or points are lost (punishment) for behaviors like fighting or rule infractions. Punishment alone is never the most effective method of changing delinquent behavior. At times it might be used in combination with other more effective social learning principles like positive reinforcement and modeling—especially if the goal is to teach behavior that is more acceptable and adaptive in the long run.

SUMMARY

Knowledge of the principles of social learning is basic for understanding both how delinquent behavior develops (is learned) and how it can be changed (unlearned). In this chapter four basic social learning principles were presented along with examples of how each is utilized first to learn delinquent behavior and then in helping delinquents change.

1. *If a consequence or result of a behavior has the effect of increasing the strength or frequency of that behavior, then POSI-*

TIVE REINFORCEMENT has taken place. Positive reinforcement (commonly called "reward") shapes or "teaches" delinquent behavior. For example, theft is reinforced immediately by the object taken. Delinquents can be helped to change by utilizing positive reinforcement for periods when the delinquent behavior does *not* occur or for behaviors incompatible with delinquent behavior.

2. *Behavior may be learned or modified simply as a function of OBSERVING THE BEHAVIOR OF A MODEL, and by observing the consequences of the model's behavior.* Many youths learn delinquent behavior by watching others (models) do it first and then they try it themselves (imitation). Likewise, modeling and imitation can be used to teach social skills in place of or incompatible with crime.

3. *When behavior is no longer followed by reinforcement, the behavior will decrease in strength or frequency and will gradually EXTINGUISH.* If attempts at prosocial or nondelinquent behaviors do *not* meet with positive reinforcement, they will extinguish or stop. Delinquents can be helped to change by helping *remove* the very reinforcers that were keeping the behavior going.

4. *If the presentation of an aversive stimulus as the consequence of a behavior decreases the strength or frequency of that behavior, then PUNISHMENT has taken place.* Children who are exposed to extensive punishment learn to avoid those doing the punishment, learn to punish or hurt others, and do not learn what to do instead. Brief punishment (time-out or response cost) can be useful for stopping delinquent behavior, especially if positive reinforcement is then used to shape nondelinquent behavior.

The application of these principles will be referred to and modeled in the remaining chapters. The next chapter describes their application in several institutions.

READINGS

1. Bandura, A., Ross, D., & Ross, S. A. (1963). Imitation of film-mediated aggressive models. *Journal of abnormal and social psychology, 66,* 3–11.

2. Stumphauzer, J. S. (Ed.) (1973). *Behavior therapy with delinquents,* Springfield, Illinois: Charles C. Thomas.

3. Stumphauzer, J. S. (1977). *Principles of behavior modification: An introduction and training manual.* Box 1168, Venice, CA, 90291: Behaviormetrics.

CHAPTER 5

Institution Programs: Social Learning in Juvenile Corrections

Historically, with the development of juvenile justice came differential treatment of adolescent offenders who were locked up. That is, they were separated from adults in jail and prisons and specialized institutions were set up for incarcerated delinquents: juvenile halls, detention centers, camps, and correctional institutions. There is a general belief today, with considerable evidence, that "punishing" or "rehabilitating" or "correcting" youths in such institutions does not really work if the goal is to change and improve behavior. Of course, the goal of incarceration may *not* be to improve behavior. Institutions may be used as temporary holding facilities before or after court. Or institutionalization may be motivated by a vague but historically popular belief that locking people up is just and effective punishment. However, if you recall from Chapter Four, the psychological definition of punishment stipulates that *punishment in fact decreases the behavior to which it is applied*. Incarceration as punishment often fails to meet this criterion. Another belief is that locking up delinquents will somehow "protect society." Of course this view is short sighted because the (now more experienced) juvenile will later be released to the same community.

From a social learning perspective there are two major problems with the use of institutionalization for changing delinquent behavior: (a) the youth is removed from the natural environment or community to which he or she must learn to adapt, and (b) these youths are exposed to delinquent peers who will further shape and encourage their antisocial behavior through modeling, imitation, and reinforcement. Buehler, Patterson, and Furniss (1966) studied this very phenomena in a now classic study. They recorded the behavior of delinquent girls in institutions and the consequences for prosocial or antisocial behaviors given by two groups: the staff and the other girl inmates. Quite clearly, the staff were inconsistent—alternately giving punishment and attention for delinquent behavior. The delinquent peers, on the other hand, were consistent in giving positive attention for antisocial acts (such as fighting) and punishment for prosocial behavior (e.g., talking about going to college). The delinquent peers in these institutions were running quite a sophisticated social learning program to teach delinquent behavior!

Alternatives to incarceration are described in detail in other chapters of this book. Some general readings and research on social learning or token economy programs in institutions can be found in three books: Ayllon and Azrin (1968), Cohen and Filipczak (1971), and Kazdin (1977). What social learning programs have been developed in juvenile corrections? We will now turn to several examples in institutions for delinquents and then some specific methods.

SOME SOCIAL LEARNING APPROACHES TO JUVENILE CORRECTIONS

One of the first applications of behavior modification to delinquents *in* institutions was that of Tyler (1967). In this case study he utilized tokens to radically improve the academic performance of one juvenile inmate. Tyler and Brown (1967) were among the first to demonstrate the effectiveness of time-out from positive reinforcement (see discussion of punishment in Chapter Four). In this instance they used swift, brief isolation (a few minutes) to decrease "acting up" around a billiard table in the recreation area of a boys' institution. Meichenbaum, Bowers, and Ross (1968) presented an early demonstration of the effectiveness of token reinforcement in institutional classrooms in an all too rare example of behavior modification with female delinquents. A high frequency of inappropriate classroom behavior was reduced to the level of noninstitutionalized peers through contingent reinforcement.

The most extensive early projects applying behavior modification to juvenile corrections were those carried out at the old National Training School For Boys in Washington, D.C. A creative group led by Harold Cohen (an architect/social designer/behaviorist) began with C.A.S.E.: a demonstration project in which the education of institutionalized delinquents was brought under reinforcement control in a programmed environment (Cohen, Filipczak, Bis & Cohen, 1966; Cohen & Filipczak, 1971). A little later they converted an old cottage in the facility to a "24-hour learning environment" for 41 delinquents. Over the time these juveniles were in this first token economy project significant increases were found in academic progress, and a remarkable 12 IQ point gain was demonstrated as well. In addition, social and attitudinal changes were found. There was a new pride of ownership in personal belongings and in living quarters. Discipline became no more than a minor problem; correctional officers were even removed from the day shift. Some of these seminal approaches were applied on a larger scale when the new Robert F. Kennedy Youth Center was opened in Morgantown, West Virginia. This program utilized a classification system and then differential behavioral treatments for different "types" of delinquents ("immature" vs. "neurotic" vs. "psychopathic") as well as a "level system" in which inmates would work their way up from "trainee" to "apprentice" to "honor student." Karacki and Levinson (1970) reported a generally positive beginning for the program. Subsequently, it appears that less and less of a token economy was maintained and the reasons are unclear. One development in the 1970's was increasing criticism of institutional programs and media sensationalization of abuses of behavior therapy with adult convicts (see Stumphauzer, 1981).

A second major project applying social learning approaches to juvenile corrections has been the program in the California Youth Authority (CYA) (Jesness & DeRisi, 1973; Jesness, 1975; Jesness, 1976). It seemed an ideal experimental design. The staff of one large CYA institution was trained in behavior modification; the staff of a second was trained in transactional analysis. Youths were thereafter randomly assigned to one or the other. Programs were maintained and multiple measures were utilized. The final results (still coming in) are less than satisfying—expecially to those betting on the "contest" of which program would "win." Both of these programs produced somewhat better results (33% recidivism) than "regular" comparison programs (42% recidivism), but these two differed little from each other. This is a gross oversimplification of a study utilizing literally hundreds of measures. It has been noted that some of the transactional analysis groups were in fact utilizing points (token reinforcement) and, therefore, the otherwise "clean" experimental design was unfortunately confounded (Stumphauzer, 1981a).

Another example of changing delinquent behavior *in* institutions is a project in a juvenile hall setting reported by Allison, Kendall, and Sloane (1979). There are a large number of juvenile halls, detention centers, and holding facilities for children and adolescents. Because youths are held only briefly while waiting for court, placement, or because there is no other placement, few programs for behavior improvement are attempted. Any treatment in these facilities seems impossible due to the short stay, crowded conditions, and largely custodial staff. In this program two behavior modification programs were compared: (a) a token or point economy system in which youths earned points for behavior improvement and (b) a phase level system in which youths earned their way through levels by meeting specified criteria in each of six performance areas (school performance, general rules, major rules, dining hall conduct, grooming, and room care). Results suggest that the level system was more effective than the token economy system. As far as cost-effectiveness it should be noted that this new program cost a little more *per day* than longer term placements, but the cost *per youth* was less because the program resulted in relatively shorter confinement.

In England, Reid (1982) reported the on-going development of a behavioral program in a secure youth treatment center. They started with a highly structured token economy but the program has evolved since its beginning in 1978 to a more flexible system with youths gradually working their way toward release and community re-entry. The program has also moved toward the delinquents' direct involvement in program changes, selection of reinforcers, etc.

Other noteworthy trends are a general shift from external control by staff to self-control by inmates, the development of "self-government" programs, and peer-managed token economies. For example, Wood and Flynn (1978) demonstrated the superiority of self-administered reinforcement over the more usual externally (other people) imposed token system. Also, Bedell and Archer (1980) showed that a peer-managed token economy could be as effective as that run by professional staff and that there were fewer social problems.

PARTICULAR METHODS IN INSTITUTIONS

1. Reinforcers in Institutions

In token economies or point systems in institutions, there are two general categories of reinforcers: (a) the token or point or "money" and (b) the "back-up reinforcers" which are literally the reinforcers that can be exchanged for or back up the tokens. Points are (forgive me) pointless if they can't be traded in for other things youths want, just as dollar bills themselves are useless if you cannot spend them. In the California Youth Authority (CYA) token economy described by Jesness and DeRisi (1973), they printed their own "dollars" which, in this instance, were the "tokens" that youths had to earn in this token economy. A copy of this "dollar" is reproduced in Figure 3. Each institution, or program within an institution, must establish a list of "back-up" reinforcers. Several factors come into play: (a) What reinforcers are available? (b) Is it ethical and/or legal to ask the youths to "earn" this privilege (e.g., a "nice" room), or is it a basic human right? (c) Can the institution afford these reinforcers? (d) Will the youths actually work (change their behavior) for *these* particular reinforcers? Obviously, input from the delinquents themselves is helpful. Figure 4 presents the "Menu" (list of back-up reinforcers and "prices") used in the special classroom of this CYA token economy.

2. Behavioral Contracts in Institutions

Increasingly in the 1970s and 1980s, behavioral contracting has been utilized *inside* institutions. This had been more common in

FIGURE 3. Token economy "dollar".

MENU

Pad of Paper	$150	Outside classes (tuition)	$200
(Paper (10 sheets)	$10	Book rental (per period)	$1
Large brown envelopes	$50	Desk (per period)	$1
Small white envelopes	$20	Floor space only (per period)	$1
Eraser rental	$1	Rest room	$5
Eraser purchase	$50	*WORK HALF-HOUR*	
Pencil rental (per period)	S1	*WITH NO CHECKS*	
Pencil purchase	$25	Sleeping	$150
Paper notebook	$50	Non-task activity	$25
Magazines	$25	Library (25 minutes)	S25
Pencil cap eraser	$10	Coffee	$35
Ink pen	$100	Deposit on coffee cup	$10
Pen refill	$50	Smoke breaks (10 minutes)	$10
Pencil clip	$25	Smoke break deposit	$5
Transcript review	$350	Tea	$35
Raffle tickets	Price varies	Sugar	$5
Chair (per period)	$1	Coffeemate®	$5
Desk & chair (monthly)	$35	Coffee refill	$15
Book Rental (monthly)	$15		

FIGURE 4. Menu of "back-up" reinforcers.

clinics (Chapter Ten), in families (Chapter Six), and in probation (Chapter Eight). The general belief, and some supporting data, suggests that teenagers are more likely to change and be less "resistant" if they have some say in their program, if they help decide what to change, and if *they* sign a contract spelling all this out. In Figure 5 you will find a sample contract, again from the CYA token economy described by Jesness and DeRisi (1973). In this instance the contract specifies behavior and "pay" earned within the Arts and Crafts program for one boy on 1-14-71. The humorous "legal seal" and simple but clear format may have added to the success of these contracts.

3. Training Correctional Officers

Obviously, comprehensive token economies, level systems, or behavioral contracting cannot be carried out in institutions unless the staff are well trained and motivated to utilize these methods. The most comprehensive behavioral training program for correctional officers has been carried out over several years by John McKee and Michael Milan at the Draper Correctional Center in Elmore, Alabama (focusing, however, on adult convicts). This training

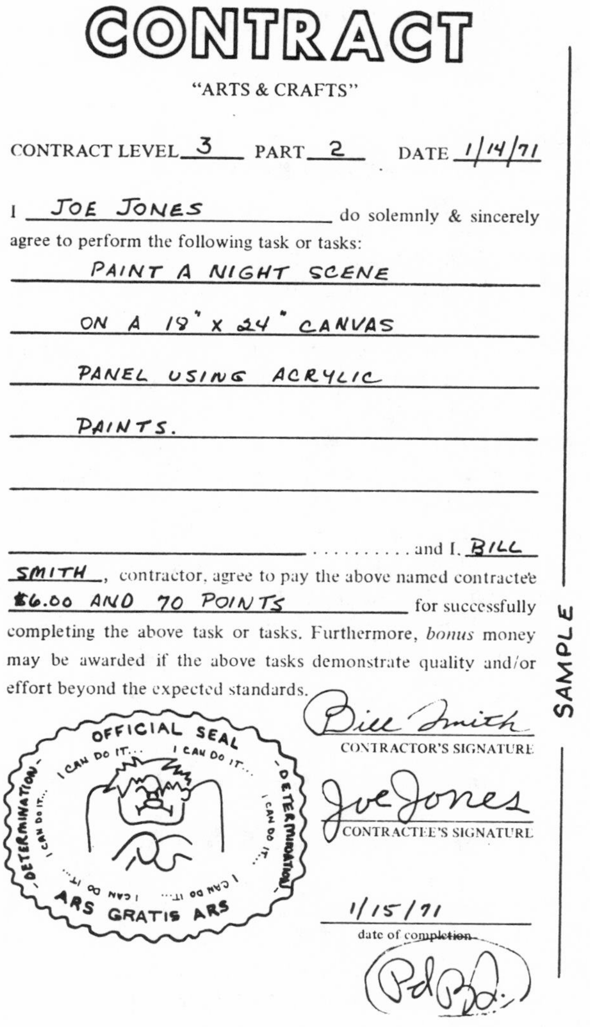

CONTRACT

"ARTS & CRAFTS"

CONTRACT LEVEL __3__ PART __2__ DATE __1/14/71__

I __JOE JONES__ do solemnly & sincerely agree to perform the following task or tasks:

__PAINT A NIGHT SCENE__

__ON A 18" X 24" CANVAS__

__PANEL USING ACRYLIC__

__PAINTS.__

_____

_____ . . . . and I, __BILL__

__SMITH__, contractor, agree to pay the above named contractee __$6.00 AND 70 POINTS__ for successfully completing the above task or tasks. Furthermore, *bonus* money may be awarded if the above tasks demonstrate quality and/or effort beyond the expected standards.

SAMPLE

OFFICIAL SEAL
ARS GRATIS ARS

Bill Smith
CONTRACTOR'S SIGNATURE

Joe Jones
CONTRACTEE'S SIGNATURE

__1/15/71__
date of completion

FIGURE 5. Contract in a youth center token economy.

program is reported by Smith, Milan, Wood, and McKee (1976) and this group has also published a number of manuals and measures for use in such training. Unfortunately, no such program is available for those working with institutionalized juveniles although this program could be used with some modifications. Officers in the Draper program were trained in three hour sessions, three days a week on the following topics:

a. an historical review of corrections;
b. identifying, defining, observing, recording and graphing behavior;
c. positive reinforcement and punishment;
d. time-out, escape and avoidance;
e. extinction and stimulus control;
f. schedules of reinforcement; and
g. shaping, chaining, and fading.

Finally, practicum exercises were conducted after completion of the formal classroom teaching so that officers could both practice what they had learned and receive feedback and supervision. The author's training manual, *Behavior Modification Principles: An Introduction And Treatment Manual* (Stumphauzer, 1977), might be used as well for training of institutional staff. Its format is introduction, history and issues in behavior modification, followed by twenty-two chapters on various principles: programmed instruction, examples with children, examples with adults, and "practice page" for the trainee to apply each principle. Reports of this manual's use with probation officers (Burkhart, Behles & Stumphauzer, 1976) and mental health personnel (Stumphauzer & Davis, 1983a, 1983b) are available.

4. Social Skills and Assertion Training in Institutions

Increasingly over the last several years programs utilizing mainly *positive* behavior influence (positive reinforcement, self-control, and modeling) have become more widely used both because they avoid the legal/ethical issues of restrictive methods utilizing pain or punishment, and they appear quite effective. Social skills training is one such approach and the program described in detail in Chapter Seven should be reviewed with an eye to applying it *inside* institutions. A related program, often subsumed today under the more general heading of social skills training, is assertion training. In general the view is that delinquents often get into trouble for being aggressive (fighting, taking) and do not know the social skill we call *assertion—standing up for your rights and getting what you want without taking away the rights of others.* Shoemaker (1979) reported assertion training programs for delinquents inside institutions. For example, in one eight week series of group assertion training meetings tokens were given for the following behaviors:

a. *Feeling talk*—"I get uptight when . . . " or "I feel very angry . . . " or "That makes me feel very happy . . . "
b. *Thinking talk*—stating likes and dislikes, agreeing or disagreeing, giving compliments.
c. *Problem talk*—talking about problems, giving suggestions about how to solve problems.
d. *Practicing*—in group role-playing or rehearsing how to handle difficult problems.

Didactic material during these sessions focused on being more assertive, becoming more "gutsy" while *not* being aggressive. Shoemaker (1979) also added a concept called "Mental Kung-Fu" adopted for its catchiness and the popularity of martial arts among boys. Three concepts were stressed:

a. *Stand tall*—acting assertive and claiming one's rights, taking responsibility;
b. *Think smart*—thinking about the consequences of one's own behavior; and
c. *Be self-controlled*—behavior is *self* directed and not directed by others.

The use of reinforcers, mild punishment (e.g., time-out from positive reinforcement), officer training programs, social skills training, and assertion training remain as viable, humane program alternatives inside institutions for delinquents.

SUMMARY

In this chapter the application of social learning approaches to helping delinquents change in institutions was reviewed. Incarceration in institutions, the most common form of intervention is, in itself, not very effective in changing delinquent behavior. Incarceration may even foster further delinquent behavior through exposure and influence of new delinquent peer models.

Several programs which have applied social learning principles in juvenile corrections were reviewed. Trends toward self administered and peer-managed token economics were noted. Sections of some institutions have been altered to become "24 hour learning environments." Classrooms in institutions have utilized social learning programs to improve academic performance and behavior. Institutional staff have been trained to apply social learning principles and to assess behavior change. Positive reinforcement (tokens or points), self-control training, and modeling have been used to help delinquents change. Contracts or signed agreements have been applied as well.

Finally, a program to teach appropriate assertion skills (deficient in some delinquent youth) in one institution was reviewed. Rather than utilize aggression (which may have resulted in trouble and incarceration) youths were taught to "stand tall" (be assertive, take responsibility), "think smart" (think of behavior consequences), and to "be self-controlled" (be self-directed and reinforce yourself).

Social learning principles have also been applied extensively in working with families. Variations of this behavioral family contracting are presented in the next chapter.

READINGS

1. Cohen, H. L., & Filipczak, J. (1971). *A new learning environment.* San Francisco: Jossey-Bass.

2. Kazdin, A. E. (1977). *The token economy.* New York: Plenum.

3. Jesness, C. F., & DeRisi, W. J. (1973). Some variations in techniques of contingency management in a school for delinquents. In J. S. Stumphauzer (Ed.) *Behavior therapy with delinquents.* Springfield, IL: Thomas. pp. 196–235.

CHAPTER 6

Behavioral Family Contracting: Helping Families Change

As we have seen in earlier chapters, the family plays a key role in the child's development. Certain methods of parenting or childrearing can change or even prevent delinquent behavior. Generally, the younger the child, the greater the influence of the family. In adolescence the family often plays less of a role and the peer group may have the greater influence. In part, this is necessary for healthy human development as young people prepare themselves to become independent adults. Often with delinquent youth, however, something has gone wrong in this process. They may not have had consistent parenting from which to learn stability when they were young children, the family may be losing even its limited influence on the child in adolescence, and peers may be shaping or "teaching" delinquent behavior through modeling and reinforcement. By the time we see families of delinquent children in the clinic, counseling session, or probation office they often have taken years to "fall apart" and become ineffective systems. These families are frequently chaotic; the adolescent is labeled "bad" or "out of control." The parents often report "we have tried everything but nothing works." In fact, as Stuart (1970) and other researchers have found, the parents have not tried everything but rather have used punishment as a parenting approach and inconsistently at that. See Chapter Four for a discussion of why punishment alone doesn't work. In these families there are no rules or agreements spelled out; no consistent demands or expectations (antecedents); and no follow-through, especially no positive reinforcement (consequences). Coming home very late may result in nothing one night and a family fight followed by "nagging" the next night.

Many times this chaotic family process can be reversed through a social learning process called behavioral family contracting.

A behavioral family contract is a formal agreement (often spelled out on paper) *which gives the family the very thing it is lacking: a specific plan and method for changing behavior in this family today.* The goal is usually a *series* of agreements between the youth, his or her family, and often others (such as teacher or probation officer) that will change behavior. The program is based on reciprocal rewards ("If you will do this . . . we will do that . . . "). Behavioral family contracting gives families four things they didn't have before:

1. structure: family members will know what behavior is expected from each other and, perhaps for the first time, what results to expect;
2. learning: a system of natural rewards and punishments arranged to maximize change or the learning of more productive behavior for the youth and more effective family interactions;
3. commitment: families who reach agreements and sign their names to them are more committed to change: "there *is* something we can do about our problems and this contract is it;"
4. responsibility: in contracting it becomes clear where the responsibilities for change lay: in the family; it is no longer "it is his fault" or "please doctor, fix my kid," but "*we* need to do this and this *today.*"

A major aspect of this approach should be underscored—the adolescent does have a say in the contracting as an "equal partner" and his or her wishes and wants are respected (perhaps an unusual event!). Remember, we are not forcing change but rather are helping the delinquent change. The therapist or counselor takes the role of *negotiator* and this is where the "art" of contracting comes in. Skill and experience (together what I meant by "art") are required to achieve a balance in each family meeting so that the parents *and* youth get what they want, the youth does not feel "ganged up on," so that compromises can in fact be reached, and the family keeps coming to sessions. This sounds like a formidable task—it is, but it can be done.

In the beginning the counselor/negotiator may have to side somewhat with the adolescent, to underscore their rights to "a point of view," and otherwise to reinforce his or her assertiveness (speaking up without taking away the rights of others). This helps considerably in avoiding "resistance" and noncompliance. The following is an example of such a negotiation session between a therapist, a seventeen year old boy and his parents.

SAMPLE NEGOTIATION OF A FAMILY CONTRACT

Therapist: So one of the problems is what time Bill comes in at night . . .

Mother: Yes, we tell him to be home early and we never know when he'll come in.

Bill: Not always.

Father: No, not always, but you come in when *you* feel like it.

T: Is there any set rule of when Bill is to be in on weekday nights and weekend nights that you all have agreed is fair?

F: There isn't much we agree on.

M: No, there's no rule but he knows I worry and want him home at a decent hour so he won't get in trouble again.

T: Let's work on this together today. Let's see if we can come up with hours for Bill to come in that are acceptable to all of you.

B: Acceptable to me?

T: Acceptable to you *and* your parents.

B: It won't do any good, they won't listen.

T: They're listening now. Do you all think there should be a different time to be home on weeknight and weekend nights?

B: Definitely *late* on weekends.

F: I guess there should be a difference.

M: Well, yes, school nights should be earlier.

T: Well, we have agreed on that already! You all think Bill should be home earlier on week nights than on weekends. Now, let's get more specific. What time should the hours be?

B: One o'clock on weekends.

F: Out of the question! A seventeen year old should not be out that late.

T: Your father doesn't think *that* is quite fair or acceptable.

M: I don't either. Eleven-thirty is late enough.

B: No way! You can't do anything and be home on a Saturday by eleven-thirty. Some parties don't start until ten.

T: Well, let's see if we can work out a compromise here. Bill, what would be a compromise that you could live with. Perhaps, one late night a weekend? What do *you* think is fair?

B: Midnight one weekend night.

F: Too late. Eleven-thirty is late enough.

T: It seems to me that many seventeen year olds are permitted to stay out *one* weekend night, but let's come back to that. Bill, would you be willing to come in by 10:00 *every* weekday night *in order to earn the privilege* of staying out until 12:00 on Friday *or* Saturday.

B: I think so, yeah.

T: *Don't agree to it unless you will really do it.*

B: Yeah, *I'd* do it, but *they* won't go for it.

T: Maybe they will. You won't be staying out too late, and they will know when to expect you home.

T: Now, what do you two think of this. Would you agree to this compromise?

M: Well, I don't know.

F: What if he didn't stick to it?

T: If he is later than 10:00 on weekday nights, then he couldn't stay out late on either weekend night. But he has already agreed he would do it.

M: I think we would be willing to try it. It would be the first time we agreed on anything in a long time.

F: Yes, ok, *if* he will do it.

T: Bill, you agree to this plan?

B: Yeah.

T: Bill will be doing what you want and Bill, you will get what you want. It sounds like a pretty fair exchange to me. Now let's put it on paper and sign it before we finish today and you and your parents will get copies to take with you. Then next week we will talk about how it worked, but I think this family is off to a good start already!

Effective family contracts should contain some basic ingredients—each of which adds an important aspect. The six important basic ingredients are:

1. The *date* the agreement is made.

2. A *general agreement*—a simple statement that the people involved agree to work together on such a program. Without it, the contract won't work because it is one-sided or coercion or perhaps no one really wants to do it. With it you have alliance, partners who

are problem solving, and motivation. Achieving this general agreement is most important and may even take a whole first family meeting to negotiate. Only *after* a general agreement is achieved should you move on to the specific "who will exchange what" below.

3. The *specific privileges* or rewards are placed on one side of the contract. These are the activities or things the adolescent wants (like "staying out until midnight on weekends," "use of the car one night a week," "$5.00 a week," etc.). It is best to write these in this way: "In order to stay out until 12:00 on Fridays and Saturdays . . . "

4. The *specific responsibilities* that go with or are linked to each privilege are spelled out in detail. Note that these are often the things the parents want, their rewards as determined in the counseling session. The counselor/negotiator must help the family arrive at specific responsibilities that are acceptable to all parties: asking for "enough" to satisfy parents without asking for so much from the teenager that he or she won't do it. Each completes the "In order to . . . " sentence started in privileges with " . . . I agree to . . . " For example, "In order to stay out until midnight on Friday and Saturday nights . . . I agree to go to school every day the week before."

5. Who is to *keep a record* of the behaviors? A form may be posted on the ever-popular refrigerator door and the adolescent may "sign in," bring notes from school, or a parent may keep a chart on each behavior. Measurement, as seen in Chapter Three, *is* critical. The record should then be brought in to the next contracting session to see what worked, what didn't, and what may need to be adjusted in a new contract for continuing success and improvement.

6. Finally, *signatures* of all involved should be added at the bottom. This adds to the commitment and responsibility of each party and shows that each really does agree to the contract, to do these things now. You may want to add your signature for further emphasis, a "legal seal," or whatever might add to the contract's importance. Others involved, such as teachers or probation officers, might add their signatures as well. Carbon or photocopies should be made for each party (one for your records) and suggestion made that it is to be posted at home—the refrigerator door is a good "public" place, but the teenager's bulletin board is another good location.

SOME EXAMPLES OF BEHAVIORAL FAMILY CONTRACTING

Behavioral contracting with families of delinquents appears to have begun about 1970. Since that time there have been many published reports. Applications have differed somewhat and results have varied with programs, measures, and settings.

An early report by Stuart (1971) presented extensive rationale and a case example. Two important assumptions he underscored were (a) that in interpersonal exchanges, receipt of a reward is a privilege rather than a right, and (b) effective contracts are governed by *reciprocity* (that something is exchanged for something). The case involved a 16 year old girl (with extensive history of delinquent behavior) and her family. The detailed contracting, carried out in the home, focused on exchanging privileges of going out (places and hours) for letting parents know where she was and returning home on time. Noteworthy is the use of natural *bonuses* (extra privileges for completing the contract or for several successful compliances) and sanctions (punishments "fitting the crime" like "If she is 10 minutes late one night . . . she must come in 10 minutes early the next"). The family contracting worked very well in this difficult case. However, after treating 79 families, Stuart and Lott (1972) questioned whether successful contracting depended upon the characteristics of contracts, clients, or therapists. They suggested that the counselor's skill in encouraging compromises may be as important, or even more important, than the actual paper document.

Alexander and Parsons (1973) appear to have further emphasized this point in a form of behavioral family contracting which focused on "reciprocity of communication." Specifically, they described the contracting as: "therapists actively modeled, prompted, and reinforced in all family members: (a) clear communication of substance as well as feelings, and (b) clear presentation of 'demands' and alternative solutions; all leading to (c) negotiation, with each family member receiving some privilege for each responsibility assumed, to the point of compromise" (p. 220). Their program was successful with a large number of families of delinquents—more successful than a "client centered" approach or a "no treatment" control group. Success of contracting was demonstrated both by improvements in family interactions as well as in lower rates of recidivism by the adolescents.

Robin and Foster (in press) have combined problem-solving with communication training in their approach to therapy with the families of adolescents. They regard families as social systems which are held together by bonds of affection and exercising mutual control over each other's contingency arrangements and behavior. Problem-solving, also utilized in the social skills training program described in Chapter Seven, here involved the following steps:

1. defining the problem (e.g., adolescent or parent behavior which causes disagreements);
2. listing the solutions (generating alternatives);
3. evaluation of alternatives (looking at and weighing possible consequences); and
4. planning and carrying out the best solution.

Communication training stressed the clear expression of opinions in assertive but nonoffensive ways, listening to and "decoding" messages from other family members, and reflection of thoughts and feelings (through verbal acknowledgements and body posture). In this approach as well, the therapist was teacher, negotiator, and source of social reinforcement.

A case simulation practice manual called *Writing Behavioral Contracts* has been developed by DeRisi and Butz (1975) who have extensive experience with such programs in the California Youth Authority (CYA) institutions. The manual is recommended reading for "where to begin," gathering data, negotiating, "trouble shooting," and practicing the skill of behavioral family contracting. In one sample contract a youth's agreement to take part in two thirty minute role playing sessions that week was exchanged for discussion of any subject of the youth's choice for thirty minutes following each session. In another sample contract if the boy attended at least three of his assigned classes each day that week, then he would be allowed to work in a store for three hours a day at two dollars an hour. To this second contract a "bonus pass" good for a hamburger and soft drink was added for every two classes over the fifteen specified in the contract for a week. Also, a penalty was added: if the boy missed more than two days of school he would lose his weekend late-night privileges for one week.

Another such program has been developed as an adjunct to the Dallas Police Department—the Youth Services Program reported by Douds, Engelsgjerd, and Collingwood (1977). Behavioral family contracting has been utilized routinely for 1200 youths and their families. Notable results based on follow-ups are that 74% of youths improved in following rules at home, 72% improved in communicating with parents, 63% did better in school attendance, and 45% increased participation in organized activities. Of the 1200 completing the program only 10.7% have been arrested (compared to 42.7% in a control group).

Behavioral contracting has been used successfully not only with families, as presented in this chapter, but also in probation (Chapter Eight), schools (Chapter Nine), employment programs (Chapter Eleven), and in group homes (Chapter Twelve).

APPLICATION OF BEHAVIORAL FAMILY CONTRACTING: CONTRACTING FORM AND TWO CASE EXAMPLES

A sample contract form, similar to that used by Stuart (1971), is provided in Table 10. It can be used with families or contracts can be written out by hand. At times it is best to have the adolescent write the contract in their own handwriting. They may have more commitment to it. Two case examples from the author's work with families of problem youth follow.

1. Steve

Steve, a 15 year old, was referred to our mental health clinic by probation following a "breaking and entering" and "vandalism" of his own school. Initially, he attended ten sessions of the social skill training program described in detail in Chapter Seven. While he successfully completed that program, it became clear that there were conflicts between he ("She bugs me. She's crazy. She won't even let me use the telephone.") and his mother ("I worry about him. I worry he will get in trouble again. He's on the telephone too long— until I yell at him."). The following contract (Table 11 developed during the first family meeting, focused on a mutual concern (telephone use) and a compromise was negotiated. Steve said, "It will never work; she will never change." Both agreed and the simple agreement seems to have made a big difference in this family. A week later they were both pleased (and surprised) at the success: "Doctor, it's amazing . . . the phone rings, he picks up the clock, talks, and when ten minutes are up he says 'I have to go

Table 10

date_____

B E H A V I O R A L   C O N T R A C T

PRIVILEGES	RESPONSIBILITES
GENERAL CONTRACT: In order to	we agree to

SPECIFIC CONTRACTS:

1. In order to	1._____agrees to
2. In order to	2._____agrees to
3. In order to	3._____agrees to
4. In order to	4._____agrees to

Bonuses and Sanctions:

Who will measure what:

SIGNATURES: _____

_____

_____

now'!'' At this point I turned to Steve, said "great, and saying 'I have to go now' and ending the telephone conversation is what I call being assertive" (something he learned in the social skills group), and he smiled in approval. In fact, at six month follow-up this agreement was still working.

2. Tammy

Tammy, a twelve year old, was referred to the clinic by her parochial school for "repeated and uncontrolled stealing" over the last five years. This case is reported in detail elsewhere

(Stumphauzer, 1976b). The following family contract (Table 12) was negotiated after a behavioral analysis (Chapter Three) determined that stealing was heavily reinforced by teacher and parent attention, little or no reinforcement was given for either "good behavior" or periods of not stealing, and all agreed to work together in improving the family (a general contract).

The behavioral family contract (with this key shift in reinforcement), combined with self-control training (Chapter Ten), resulted in an almost immediate cessation of stealing. Stealing did not occur again over eighteen months of follow-up while productive, nondelinquent behavior increased.

Table 11

FAMILY CONTRACT ON TELEPHONE USE

CONTRACT

date: 4-29-85

GENERAL AGREEMENT: In order to imrove things   the family, we agree to work on a program together.

SPECIFIC CONTRACT

SPECIFIC PRIVILEGES	SPECIFIC RESPONSIBILITIES
1. In order to use the telephone and not have his mother "bug him" while he is on the telephone ...	1. Steve agrees to use the telephone (calls in or out) for only 10 min. each time.

RECORD

Mrs. W. will keep a record of telephone use (approx. min. per call each day) and bring it in next week.

SIGNATURES

Steve
_____
Mrs. W
_____
Dr. J.
_____

Table 12

date **May 6**

B E H A V I O R A L   C O N T R A C T

PRIVILEGES	RESPONSIBILITES
GENERAL CONTRACT:	
In order to...	we agree to...
help Tammy stop stealing	**work together on this program.**

SPECIFIC CONTRACTS:

1. In order to **get 20¢ for icecream...**

1. **Tammy** agrees /**not** to **steal or borrow in school the day before.**

2. In order to

2. _____ agrees to

3. In order to

3. _____ agrees to

4. In order to

4. _____ agrees to

Bonuses and Sanctions:
As a bonus, Tammy will get special Sunday pancakes...if she does not steal or borrow in school all week.

Who will measure what: **Tammy will carry DAILY BEHAVIOR CARD back and forth to school; she will count number of times she steals and Sister Louise will countersign the card if she agrees with the count.**

SIGNATURES: _____**Tammy**_____

_____**Therapist**_____   _____**Mr. and Mrs. P.**_____

_____**Sister Louise**_____

SUMMARY

Families play a key role in child development (including delinquency) and families, as presented in this chapter, can help delinquents change. Behavioral family contracting refers to the application of the social learning approach in a series of family agreements or contracts.

The counselor or therapist takes the role of negotiator and teacher, helps the family understand delinquent behavior, and helps provide and negotiate a specific plan for changing behavior in that family starting that day. Behavioral family contracting provides structure, a natural system for learning and changing, commitment (signed agreements), and responsibility (in effect, the family agrees to change itself).

Ideally, each family contract contains key ingredients: that day's date, a general agreement to work together, specific privileges (reinforcers or rewards), specific responsibilities linked to each privilege, a system of record keeping (assessment), and signatures of all involved. For example, a privilege such as "use of the family car one night a week" could be exchanged for a responsibility such as "agree to attend school every day the week before." At times one contract can help a family change delinquent behavior, but more often a series of contracts are necessary as behavior changes and as other problems are worked on. Others have combined behavioral contracting with family communication training. A negotiation transcript, a contracting form, and two case examples from the author's work were presented.

Social learning principles have been applied to delinquents in groups to teach behavior incompatible with youth crime. This social skills training approach is described in the following chapter and one program is presented in detail.

READINGS

1. Alexander, J. F., & Parsons, B. V. (1973). Short-term behavioral intervention with delinquent families: Impact on family process and recidivism. *Journal of Abnormal Psychology, 81,* 219–225.

2. De Risi, W. J., & Butz, G. (1975). *Writing behavioral contracts: A case simulation practice manual.* Champaign, IL: Research Press.

3. Robin, A. L., & Foster, S. L. (in press). *Parent-adolescent problem solving and communication.* New York: Guilford.

CHAPTER 7

Social Skills Training:
Teaching Behaviors Incompatible
with Crime

Delinquents lack social skills. Delinquents are too socially skilled. Which statement is correct? Probably both. Some delinquents may appear only too skillful at manipulating others, lying, bullying and being aggressive rather than assertive. Yet these same delinquents may lack many *adaptive* social skills such as getting a job, keeping a job, speaking up, problem-solving, and being assertive rather than aggressive (standing up for their own rights without taking away the rights of others). Many other young people do not fit the socially manipulative delinquent stereotype at all. They may have committed solitary violations like theft, vandalism, or individual acts of violence. In addition to the social skills already mentioned, they may be lacking in basic social abilities like listening to others, talking to members of the opposite sex, joining in with members of their own age group, asking for things they want, and telling people when they are displeased.

We may define social skills as social behaviors necessary to insure successful social interactions such as conversation skills, assertiveness, and expressing approval/disapproval. Agryle (1969) viewed these skills like other abilities and suggested that they were indeed teachable. In the last fifteen years there has been ample evidence that such skills can be behaviorally analyzed, taught, and learned by adults, children and adolescents. Falloon, Lindley, McDonald, and Marks (1977), for example, demonstrated that social skills could be successfully taught to adult psychiatric patients. A review of social skills training with children found a number of methodological problems that prevented definitive conclusions at the time (Van Hasselt, Hersen, Whitehill & Bellack,

1979). There are several readings that can be consulted. LeCroy (1983) has edited a book on social skills training for children and youth. Three books or manuals have been published to help counselors train children and adolescents in social skills (Spence, 1980; Cartledge & Milburn, 1980; Goldstein, Sprafkin, Gershaw, & Klein, 1980).

SOME EXAMPLES OF SOCIAL SKILLS TRAINING WITH DELINQUENTS

A number of studies have focused on social skills training with convicted delinquents (Spence, 1979). For the most part this research is encouraging in showing that social skills training can be taught to young offenders. The more difficult question is whether social skills training can, in fact, reduce or prevent further delinquent behavior. An additional problem is that most of these projects have been carried out with young people *inside* institutions and relatively few attempts have been made to increase the chances of generalization by teaching social skills to delinquents in the community where their newly acquired social abilities could be utilized and reinforced naturally. Once again, most of the work has been carried out with young male offenders and little is known about social skills training with female delinquents.

A major, three-part program focusing on one important set of social skills—assertion—has been reported by Shoemaker (1979). Shoemaker increased appropriate assertive behavior in groups of delinquents in a boys' residential center with use of discussion, modeling, social and token reinforcement, and especially innovative and attractive techniques such as "Mental Kung Fu." Assertive behavior did generalize from the training sessions to a "test social situation" (an interview with a "pushy" counselor), but no assessment of transfer of learning to post-release was made.

Susan Spence has reported a number of social skills training projects with young, male offenders in England, and her particular techniques are reported in a recommended manual for counselors (Spence, 1980). In a multiple baseline design, Spence and Marzillier (1979) found relative ease in teaching certain social skills like eye-contact to young offenders, but that some "listening skills" were more difficult to teach. Spence and Spence (1980) focused on cognitive changes in institutionalized delinquents concurrent with social skills training, attention-placebo, or no treatment. While social skills training appeared to increase self-esteem and internal locus of control (the belief that one controls one's own behavior), the effects were short-lived. Finally, Spence (1981) validated social skills of young male offenders by utilizing four judges who viewed video tapes of conversation with a previously unknown adult.

Ollendick and Hersen (1979) also reported a program teaching social skills to institutionalized male delinquents. The program consisted of ten weekly sessions of instruction, feedback, modeling, behavior rehearsal, social reinforcement and graduated homework assignments. This training was more effective than discussion and control groups on several measures.

One of the few programs carried out with noninstitutionalized delinquents (which focused exclusively on employment training) will be reviewed in detail in Chapter Eleven. In that program, Mills and Walter (1979) not only trained delinquents in job-related social skills, but also trained employers how to naturally reward such skills in these youths.

A community-based project has been reported which combined behavior modification, social skills training, and self-management training for male and female court referred youths (Gross, Brigham, Hopper, & Bologira, 1980). Decreases were found in number of problem behaviors at home and at school, and the youths judged the program effective in a consumer evaluation.

Social skills training is also a key component of occupational skills training (Chapter Eleven) and can be utilized one-on-one in clinical behavior therapy (Chapter Ten). A program developed for teenagers on probation is described in detail below.

SOCIAL SKILLS TRAINING
FOR ADOLESCENTS ON PROBATION:
LEARNING TO STAY OUT OF TROUBLE

A specialized program for adolescents currently on probation has been developed at the Child Psychiatry Clinic of the Los Angeles County—University of Southern California Medical Center by the author. Five developments led to the current program: (a) the author's long-standing interest in social learning approaches to delinquency, (b) recent financial and staff cut-backs in the Los Angeles County Probation Department resulting in minimal or no counseling of probationers (caseloads of as many as 200 children and adolescents), (c) the need (based, again, on financial concerns) within the Los Angeles County Department of Mental Health to move toward time-limited psychotherapies, (d) the need to expose predoctoral psychology interns, other trainees, and staff to innovative approaches for the treatment of delinquents, and (e) the development of social skills training as a viable treatment as demonstrated by the foregoing literature.

Referrals

Referrals were sought from the Northeast Juvenile Justice Center, the probation division that serves the immediate community surrounding the medical center: the central and eastern metropolitan area of Los Angles. The proposal to provide a special service to youths on probation was presented to the chief of that division and subsequently a meeting was held with the on-line probation officers. The author's previous work with delinquents and area youth gangs was discussed, as was the general social learning approach. It was agreed that cutbacks in probation had all but tied the officers hands in doing direct counseling of juveniles and then the current program was offered as an alternative: a time-limited (ten session) program of social skills training on "how to stay out of trouble." In response to "only ten sessions?" one officer gave a pointed reply: "But it's more than any of them will get with six months of probation!" The proposed topics (getting a job, resisting peer-pressure, being assertive rather than aggressive) were very well received and apparently a welcome contrast to traditional psychotherapy which they viewed somewhat negatively. The officers agreed to begin referring adolescent probationers to the program and were instructed as to the usual clinic referral and evaluation policy which was to be followed.

Intake Procedure

Standard clinic intake procedure was followed both for ease of administration and to provide a service that could easily be duplicated in other clinics. The adolescent probationer was required, as a condition of probation, to seek treatment at the clinic and he or his parents had to call for an intake/evaluation appointment. Routine intake evaluations (presenting problems, social history, mental status, DSM III diagnosis, and treatment plan) were conducted and written by any staff or trainees available (virtually no waiting list). Usually the following week the case was presented to the Disposition Conference team (staff psychiatrist, psychologist, and social worker) and final referral made to the specialized delinquency program.

Selection of Social Skills

Within a time-limited, ten session format it was necessary to select the most salient social skills for adolescent probationers in metropolitan Los Angeles to learn "in order to stay out of trouble." The author and two psychology interns (Laura Fogwell and Andy Blew) first determined major *problem areas:* aggression, peer-pressure to violate the law, school problems (truancy, failure, fighting), bad tempers, attitudes like "it's not my fault" and "there's no choice," anger at authorities, and unemployment. Next, a series of broadly conceived social skills were selected to solve those very problems. Each had to be simplified into teachable segments. Could these skills be taught in a clinic setting? The relevant literature was searched to see if each had been taught before and, if so, precisely how it had been done. We then adapted each to delinquents living in central Los Angeles, placed them in a reasonable sequential order, and finally settled on ten sessions of social skill training. A treatment manual, "How to Stay Out of Trouble," with a description of the content of each session, and forms used, follows below so that others can evaluate its use further. Each session is ninety minutes and follows the format: review of previous session and "homework," introduction of new topic, discussion, modeling, role-play, social reinforcement, and assignment of "homework." Whenever possible humor is incorporated into discussions and role-play but the overall seriousness of the topic is not undermined. A session-by-session description and forms used follows.

HOW TO STAY OUT OF TROUBLE: A TEN-SESSION TREATMENT MANUAL

1. How to Get Off Probation

Before the first session, premeasures are filled out by the youth and their parent. Probation is discussed and their varying "probation requirements" are clarified. Each youth is encouraged to "speak up" in a role-play session with a therapist who plays a probation officer. The "officer" goes over a seven-item checklist of fairly universal requirements (see Table 13) and hands the resulting checklist to the youth to take with him in order to make his current standing on probation requirements clear and up-to-date. Next a vote of group members is taken on: "Is he ready to get off probation? Was he lying? What did his behavior say?" The social skill of speaking-up and areas in need of improvement are underscored. "Homework" might include talking to their probation officer, parents, or focus on particular probation requirements.

2. Job Skills A: Finding a Job

Session one is reviewed and any "homework" results are discussed; progress is socially reinforced with attention and praise. Members fill out a "self-assessment for jobs" checklist of personal strong points and weak points (found in Table 14). Group members are asked why jobs are important and discussions of earning money, gaining experience, and staying out of trouble are reinforced. Next, each is asked to "tell me about yourself" (with self-assessment checklist in front of him) and to describe *any* job experience. A list of "places to look for a job" is generated on the blackboard (ask relative, ask friend who is working, school career office, etc.) and finally, for "homework," each leaves with a list

Table 13

CHECKLIST FOR GETTING OFF PROBATION

Name_____   Date_____

CHECKLIST:

1) _____ not break any laws,

2) _____ attend school every day,

3) _____ at home by curfew hour: 10:00 PM,

4) _____ obey parents,

5) _____ meet with probation officer when asked,

6) _____ attend counseling sessions,

and   7) _____ do something extra like get a job, or

sports, or volunteer in the neighborhood.

Table 14

SELF ASSESSMENT AND PLACES TO LOOK FOR A JOB

Name_____   Date_____

1. MY STRONG POINTS AND WEAK POINTS

INSTRUCTIONS: Put an "X" next to those of the following
things that describe you:

__I like to work with people	__I don´t like to work with people
__I am good with math	__I am bad with math
__I have job experience	__I have never worked
__I am handy with tools	__I am not good with tools
__I am in excellent health	__I have health problems
__I really want a job	__I have a bad back
__I am a good worker	__I don´t really want to work
__I learn things fast	__I am not a very good worker
__I can work every afternoon or evenings and weekends	__I don´t want to work weekends, nights, or some afternoons
__I would have no problem getting to work every day	__I would have trouble getting to work
__I can be trusted with money	__I can´t be trusted with money
__I can start work today	__I would like to start work sometime later
__I speak Spanish	__I am slow to learn things
__I read and write Spanish	

2. LIST THE PLACES YOU CAN LOOK FOR A JOB THIS WEEK:

1. _____   4._____

2._____   5._____

3._____

of at least three of these places or persons they agree to contact that
week.

3. Job Skills B: Job Application and Interview

Session two is reviewed and progress on job search is reinforced.
Each begins by filling out a real job application form (obtained from
McDonalds ''down the street'') with individual help on questions,
spelling, etc. (see Table 15). Next, each member takes part in a
video-taped job interview answering such questions as: ''Why do

you want this job? What is your experience? What hours can you work?'' Interviews are then played back with praise for "enthusiasm," good answers, and assertiveness. Areas in need of improvement are sometimes roleplayed again with prompts (e.g., "This time say 'I don't have any experience as a clerk . . . *but* I *am* good with numbers and I learn fast . . . I *really do* want this job.''). Homework is continuing job search and job application.

4. Job Skills C: Keeping a Job

Session three is reviewed and job applications/interviews praised. Each is asked to complete a checklist of "things that might be a

Table 15

JOB APPLICATION FORM

EMPLOYMENT APPLICATION

SOCIAL SECURITY NO _____

NAME _____ STREET ADDRESS _____
FIRST NAME   MIDDLE INITIAL   LAST NAME

APT. NO.
OR BOX _____ CITY _____ STATE _____ ZIP _____

AREA CODE _____   TEL. NO _____

ARE YOU 18 ☐ YES
OR OLDER? ☐ NO , IF NOT, AGE _____

EVER WORKED FOR McDONALD'S BEFORE?
IF YES, DATES AND LOCATION _____

AVAILABILITY:

	HOURS AVAILABLE:	M	T	W	T	F	S	S
TOTAL HOURS AVAILABLE PER WEEK _____	FROM							
	TO							

ARE YOU LEGALLY ABLE TO BE EMPLOYED IN THE U.S.? ☐ YES ☐ NO
HOW DID YOU HEAR OF JOB? _____
HOW FAR DO YOU LIVE FROM STORE? _____
DO YOU HAVE TRANSPORTATION TO WORK? _____

SCHOOL MOST RECENTLY ATTENDED:

NAME _____ LOCATION _____ PHONE _____

TEACHER OR COUNSELOR _____ DEPT. _____
LAST GRADE COMPLETED _____
GRADE POINT AVERAGE _____

GRADUATED? ☐ YES ☐ NO   NOW ENROLLED? ☐ YES ☐ NO
SPORTS OR ACTIVITIES _____

TWO MOST RECENT JOBS: (IF NOT APPLICABLE PERSONAL REFERENCES)

COMPANY _____ LOCATION _____ PHONE _____

JOB _____ SUPERVISOR _____ DATES WORKED: FROM _____ TO _____

SALARY _____ REASON FOR LEAVING _____ REFERENCE CHECK DONE BY

COMPANY _____ LOCATION _____ PHONE _____

JOB _____ SUPERVISOR _____ DATES WORKED: FROM _____ TO _____

SALARY _____ REASON FOR LEAVING _____ REFERENCE CHECK DONE BY

U.S. MILITARY:

HAVE YOU SERVED IN THE U.S. MILITARY? ☐ YES ☐ NO

PHYSICAL:

IF ANY SUCH HEALTH PROBLEMS OR PHYSICAL DEFECTS EXIST, PLEASE EXPLAIN

ANY HEALTH PROBLEMS OR PHYSICAL DEFECTS WHICH COULD AFFECT YOUR EMPLOYMENT? ☐ YES ☐ NO _____

*DURING THE PAST 10 YEARS, HAVE YOU EVER BEEN CONVICTED OF A CRIME, EXCLUDING MISDEMEANORS AND TRAFFIC VIOLATIONS? ☐ YES ☐ NO
IF YES, DESCRIBE IN FULL _____

* A conviction will not necessarily bar you from employment

1. I certify that the information contained in this application is correct to the best of my knowledge and understand that deliberate falsification of this information is grounds for dismissal in accordance with McDonald's policy. 2. I authorize the references listed above to give you any and all information concerning my previous employment and any pertinent information they may have, personal or otherwise, and release all parties from all liability for any damage that may result from furnishing same to you. 3. I understand that no representative of the company has the authority to enter into any agreement for employment for any specified period of time, nor am I obligated to work for the company for any specified period of time.

DATE _____ SIGNATURE _____

McDonald's is an equal opportunity employer. The Civil Rights Act of 1964 and State and Local laws prohibit discrimination on the basis of race, color, religion, sex or national origin. In addition, State and Local laws prohibit discrimination on the basis of disability and the Age Discrimination in Employment Act of 1978 and some State and Local laws prohibit discrimination on the basis of age with respect to individuals who are at least 40 but less than 70 years of age. It is our policy to comply fully with these Acts and information requested on this application will not be used for any purpose prohibited by law.

If you are handicapped, a disabled veteran or veteran of the Vietnam era, McDonald's invites you to voluntarily and confidentially identify yourself for equal opportunity purposes. Failure to respond will not subject you to adverse treatment, and information provided will be used only in accordance with the law and for equal opportunity purposes. ☐ Handicapped ☐ Disabled Veteran ☐ Vietnam Era Veteran

YOUR APPLICATION WILL BE CONSIDERED ACTIVE FOR 30 DAYS-FOR CONSIDERATION AFTER THAT YOU MUST REAPPLY

problem for you" developed by Mills and Walter (1979) as potential job related problems (found in Table 16). Discussion centers on these problem areas and how to problem-solve and develop solutions with a boss *without* quitting or getting fired. Each then role-plays a confrontation with a "boss" on one or more areas that he has checked for himself (e.g., "You've been late *three* times this week, what's going on?"). Problem-solving, negotiation, and assertiveness are stressed. "Homework" is further job search or keeping a job.

5. Problem-Solving: How to Make Choices

Session four is reviewed and practice at job skills and job acquisition is reinforced. A "decision chart" (adapted from Russell and Thoresen, 1976, Table 17) is started for each with a current problem (arguing with parents, failing a class, etc.). Discussion centers on "You are in control of your life," "You always have choices" and "There *are* alternatives . . . you don't have to react the way you usually do." For each youth, what they "usually" do is written on their decision chart while pointing out the good points (if any) and bad points (e.g., arguing doesn't do any good). Next, two alternatives to the problem are generated by the group (could try to talk when *not* arguing or could try *never* to raise your voice) with good and bad points of each. Finally, the youth is asked to *decide* which is the *best choice* now that he has three (usual, alternate one, and alternate two), to sign that decision, and to try *that* choice as "homework" that week. They take their decision chart with them.

6. Assertion Training A: Introduction

Session five is reviewed; utilization of new choices is praised as is further problem-solving (i.e., if *that one* didn't work, then what are other choices?). *Assertive* (standing up for your rights *without* taking away the rights of others), *nonassertive* (quiet, shy, not speaking up), and *aggressive* (taking rights of others, stealing, hitting, name-calling) are introduced by discussion and demonstration by the group leader. Aggression is discouraged because it often gets them in trouble (probably did), and assertion is encouraged as "the best way to get what you want for the rest of your life." Nonassertiveness does not "work" and leaves you "feeling dumb." Each is asked to role-play all three "ways to react" in simple situations (see Table 18). The assertive choice is praised and

Table 16

KEEPING A JOB

INSTRUCTIONS:
CIRCLE THE ONES BELOW THAT MIGHT BE A PROBLEM FOR YOU ON A JOB:

1. Be on time.

2. Be at work every scheduled day.

3. Do work expected for the job, thoroughly.

4. Dress according to employer guidelines.

5. Follow orders.

6. Cooperativeness.

7. Willingness to learn.

8. Friendliness with co-workers.

9. Friendliness with clients, custormers, tenants, etc.

10. Notify employer if going to be late or absent, well before scheduled time.

11. Take only time alloted for breaks, lunch, and only at times specified.

12. Do not use telephone during working hours.

13. Do not have friends, realatives stop in at work.

14. Interest in the organization and your part in it.

15. Get enough sleep to function well on the job.

16. No drugs or alcohol on the job, during breaks or lunch, or before work.

17. Honesty, no stealing or "borrowing" anything belonging to the the organization, no lying when you do not feel like working.

18. Little or no smoking on the job.

19. Accepting responsibility, looking for things that need to be done without having to be told, i.e., if work is finished, not sitting around.

20. Transportation to and from work planned for each day, ahead of time.

its potential success underscored. Care must be taken to minimize reinforcement for aggression (laughs, peer-approval). "Homework" is to try particular assertive solutions.

7. Assertion Training B: Talking to Authorities

Assertive, nonassertive, and aggressive are reviewed. Discussion centers on talking to police, probation officers, parents, and teachers with ways to be assertive without getting in trouble (see Table 19).

Role-play centers on each "being stopped and questioned by police" or talking to other realistic authority such as teachers. Appropriate, adaptive assertion is praised and "homework" is applying assertion skills (e.g., talk to *that* teacher *this* week).

8. Assertion Training C: How to Say "No" to Peer Pressure to Do Delinquent Behavior

Assertion concepts are reviewed, peer-pressure is discussed, and their *right* to say "no" to peers and friends is underscored. Several "ways to say no" are generated on the blackboard (Table 20). Excuses and lying ("not now, I'm busy, I'm sick") are discouraged as not working in the long run. Each role-plays three

Table 17

DECISION MAKING - PROBLEM SOLVING

Name _____   Date_____

D E C I S I O N   C H A R T

My problem is_____

1. I could do what I usually do which is_____

_____

      good point_____

      bad point_____

2. OR I could_____instead.

      good point_____

      bad point_____

3. OR I could_____instead.

      good point_____

      bad point_____

Before deciding I will need to know_____

My decision is to do number ____.

                               _____
                                   signature

Table 18

ASSERTION INSTEAD OF AGGRESSION

1) Discussion of the differences among the following with examples from the members of each:

    a) ASSERTIVE (speak up for your rights <u>without</u> hurting others)

    b) NONASSERTIVE (shy, quiet, no speaking up for your rights)

    c) AGGRESSIVE (fight, steal, hurt others)

2) Discussion of:

    a) what leads up to aggression, how you learn it,

    b) how aggression gets you in trouble,

    c) why being nonassertive doesn´t pay off, and

    d) why assertion works best.

3) Practice role-playing assertive behavior:

SITUATIONS FOR ASSERTIVENESS TRAINING WITH ADOLESCENTS:

    1. You order a cheeseburger and the waitress brings you a hamburger.

    2. You are in line and somebody cuts ahead of you.

    3. The teacher is going too fast for you.

    4. Policeman stops you and asks you what you are doing out at 11:00 PM.

    5. There is a new girl (boy) in school you would like to talk to.

    6. Somebody calls you a name.

    7. Some of your friends come by in the morning and ask you to cut school with them.

ways to say "no" to group pressure to commit a delinquency (cut school, buy stolen radio, ride in stolen car, etc.) with feedback on which sounded "weak" and which sounded effective. For "homework" they are asked to note their assertions with peers and utilization of "no" if needed.

9. Assertion Training D: How to Say "No" to Peer Pressure to Do Drugs

Assertion, ways to say "no," and "homework" are reviewed. Drugs in current use by peers are discussed. This also educates the group leaders every ten weeks! The potential harms of drugs, and substance abuse as a violation of probation, are stressed. Peer-pressure, direct ("here, try this") and subtle (being somewhere when everyone else is doing it) is discussed. Ways to say "no" are role-played with group pressure to drink alcohol or use other drugs (Table 21). Assertion and effective ways to say "no" (and still maintain respect by being seen as "strong" and "smart") are praised. "Homework" is continuing appropriate assertion with peers. Also, members are asked to self-assess two to four school-related behaviors on a Daily Behavior Card (Stumphauzer, 1974b; see Chapter Three) for the tenth session (e.g., attended school, went to football practice).

10. School Skills: How to Get Through School

Session nine is reviewed as are results on each Daily Behavior Card. Discussion centers on school attendance as one of the

Table 19

TALKING TO AUTHORITIES

1) Talking to Police:

Get the group to make out a list on the board of what "to do" and what "not to do if stopped by the police.

WHAT TO DO	WHAT NOT TO DO
1. stay cool	1. run
2. speak up	2. mumble
3. be polite ("Sir")	3. act "smart"
4. look at them when answering	4. get aggressive
5. do what they say	
6. carry I.D.	

Then get each member to role-play being stopped and questioned by police, and get peers to give feedback on how they did on the above lists.

2. Talking to teachers (discussion, modeling and role-play).

3. Talking to parents (discussion, modeling and role-play).

Table 20

BEING ASSERTIVE WITH PEERS

1) HOW TO HANDLE PEER PRESSURE: discussion of peer pressure
and how to be assertive in saying "no" if you want to.
Review why making "excuses" and "lying" don't work.
It is your <u>right</u> to say "no". Role-play pressure
to do the following with social reinforcement for
appropriate assertive approach to each:

    a) cut school,

    b) do something against the law (e.g., buying
       stolen property),

    c) fight, or

    d) get into a stolen car at a party.

2) REVIEW WAYS TO SAY "NO":

    a) just say "no" firmly and calmly,

    b) broken record: repeat it over and over
       until they get the message,

    c) offer alternative activity: "Let's
       do _____ instead",

    d) change the subject, introduce new topic,

    e) request them not to ask you: "Look, I don't
       want to do it, and <u>don't</u> ask me again."

    f) If all else fails, leave the scene: "Hey,
       I'll see you later..."

most basic probation requirements and the relative standing of each member in school is reviewed (e.g., "I'm in the tenth grade and failing math"). Problem-solving and assertive solutions to school related problems are discussed and role-played (e.g., arrange appointment with teacher to see what you can do to pass that subject, talk to school counselor about changing to a technical school with job training; see Table 22). Progress in staying out of trouble and applying these skills as steps to getting off probation are positively reinforced. Post-measures, including "Consumer Evaluation," are completed by each group member.

Measures

Traditional, everyday clinical measures were utilized wherever possible (parent and youth interview, probation reports, school reports, and session by session progress notes). In addition, at the onset and termination of treatment, Quay and Peterson's (1974) "Problem Behavior Checklist" was filled out by the parent or legal guardian. Four additional measures were developed for this program:

1. Social Skills and Social Problems,
2. SASA (Stumphauzer Assertion Scale for Adolescents, Table 7),
3. Rules and Regulations, and
4. Consumer Evaluation.

The first three are administered at intake and termination. A self-report form, "Social Skills and Social Problems" requires each youth to rate how big a problem each social skill is for him at the moment (Table 23). The SASA is a new scale designed by the author which enables adolescents to rate themselves on assertion, aggression, and nonassertion (see Chapter Three). The third scale, "Rules and Regulations," was adapted from previous research (Hindelang, Hirschi, & Weis, 1981), but here was developed as a forced-choice measure of relatively minor crimes (Table 24). Finally, in order to gauge the youth's own reaction to the program

Table 21

DEALING WITH PEER PRESSURE II: DRUG ABUSE

TOPICS OR SCENES:

1) Review ways to say "no".

2) Ask them about the various drugs used among their peers and in their schools. Check their beliefs and lead discussion of the harmful and legal aspects of each: sniffing glue/paint, alcohol, marijuana, PCP, acid, pills, cocaine, and heroin. Discuss peer pressure as it relates to drug use (both direct and subtle).

3) Practice being assertive and saying "no" to a group of friends who are trying to pressure you to use a drug. Role-play three different ways to say "no" including at least one way that is new for you to learn.

4) Discussion and role-play of being assertive in speaking up to a friend who you would like to get to stop using drugs.

5) Give them a DAILY BEHAVIOR CARD (see Chapter Three) to measure some important behaviors this coming week (include school attendance for next week's topic).

Table 22

SOCIAL SKILLS IN GETTING THROUGH SCHOOL

Utilization of Assertion and Problem-Solving in getting through school by dealing with the following areas:

1) How to graduate?

> Discuss, for each of them, steps they need to take. Is high school graduation important for later life?

2) School and probation.

> School attendance is a basic requirement of probation.

3) School attendance: why it is important.

> Daily Behavior Card for one week; go over results.

4) School problems (e.g., failing a class)

> Discuss assertion and problem-solving to deal with real situation for each. For example, role-play asking a teacher for a meeting or asking teacher for help and then negotiating solution.

5) Vocational training programs in school

> What do you need to do (assertion, problem-solving) to change to a vocational or job training program?

and to gather suggestions from each, a "Consumer Evaluation" form was developed (Table 25) and is administered at the time each completes the program.

Preliminary results with the first twenty graduates of the program (those who completed ten sessions) are quite encouraging thus far. Responses on the Consumer Evaluation by the youths were uniformly positive: 65% said they learned "a great deal," 85% said it was a "good" or "very good" program for young people on probation, and 55% said they enjoyed the meeting "a great deal." The two "most important" things they reported learning were noted as "how to fill out a job application" and "how to say 'no' to friends who might get you in trouble." Probation officers (the "consumers" who had referred these probationers), much to their surprise, have reported that these (traditionally "resistant" youths) *liked* these sessions. In fact, four of these twenty youths brought friends as "guests" to meetings with them. On the Consumer Evaluation, 100% said they "would recommend this program to others."

On the Behavior Problem Checklist, parents checked an average of nine behavior problems before social skills training; this number of concerns dropped to four after ten sessions. Likewise, there were apparent improvements on self-ratings by these twenty adolescents. Their average self-ratings on "social skills" increased from the "some problem" range to the "no problem" range. On the SASA,

Table 23

SOCIAL SKILLS AND SOCIAL PROBLEMS   Name_____
                                        date_____
HOW BIG A PROBLEM ARE THESE
THINGS FOR YOU?

DO YOU:	3 NO Problem	2 Some Problem	1 A Big Problem
1. Know how to get off probation?			
2. Know how to look for a job?			
3. Know how to fill out a job application?			
4. Know how to keep a job once you have it?			
5. Know the steps to take to solve any problem?			
6. Know how to speak up for yourself?			
7. Know how to talk your way out of a fight?			
8. Know how to talk to police, teachers and probation?			
9. Know how to say "no" to friends who try to get you to do something illegal?			
10. Know how to graduate from school?			
11. Know how to talk to members of the opposite sex?			
12. Know how to make new friends?			
13. Know how to stay out of trouble?			

Table 24

RULES AND REGULATIONS				

Name_____
date_____

INSTRUCTIONS: recent research has found that everyone breaks some rules and regualions during his lifetime. Some break them regularly, others less often. Below are some frequently broken.

CHECK THOSE THAT YOU HAVE BROKEN IN THE LAST THREE MONTHS:	1. No	2. Once or Twice	3. Several Times	4. Very Often
1. Driven a car without a driver's license or permit? (Do not include driver training class.)				
2. Skipped school without a legitimate excuse?				
3. Defied your parent's authority (to their face)?				
4. Taken little things (worth less that $2.00) that did not belong to you?				
5. Bought or drank beer, wine, or liquor? (include drinking at home.)				
6. Purposely damaged or destroyed public or private property that did not belong to you?				
7. Had sex relations with a person of the opposite sex?				
8. Had a fist fight with another person?				

Hindelang, Hirschi, Weis (1981); JSS (1982)

assertiveness self-ratings increased while those on aggression decreased. Finally, self-rating on Rules and Regulations (rule breaking and minor crimes) indicated a decrease in these activities. However, caution should be used in interpreting these findings. They are preliminary and incomplete. Statistical analysis with larger numbers of youths (compared to youths who do not complete the program) remains to be done, and decreases in arrest rates and actual crimes have not yet been fully documented. Nonetheless, at this time it would appear that ten weeks of social skills training may prove to be a promising, cost-effective alternative to traditional interventions. The "manual" and program should be evaluated by others as well. This program could be carried out in probation departments, schools, and directly in the community. An added revelation (in the delinquency treatment field) appears to be that the youths themselves like and recommend this program.

Table 25

CONSUMER EVALUATION

(Youth Evaluation Of Program)   Name_____

date_____

INSTRUCTIONS: Circle the answer you believe to be true:

1. How much did you learn from the social skills training sessions?   nothing   a little   a great deal

2. Circle the two most important things you learned from the program:
   1. how to get off probation
   2. how to find a job
   3. how to fill out an application
   4. how to be interviewed
   5. how to solve problems
   6. how to be assertive
   7. how to talk to authorities
   8. how to say "no" to friends who might get you in trouble
   9. how to have success in school

3. How effective were the staff in the program?   not effective   OK   Good   very effective

4. How much did you enjoy the meetings?   a great deal   a little   not at all

5. How much did this program help you?   not at all   a little   a great deal

6. Is this a good program for young people on Probation?   very good   good   OK   no good

7. Would you recommend this program to other young people?   no   yes

8. How would you change or imporve the program? Circle as many as you think are important.
   ^{1}have more meetings ^{2}have less meetings ^{3}meet on a different day

   ^{4}include girls ^{5}include a probation officer ^{6}talk about personal problems

   ^{7}include parents ^{8}use acting more ^{9}use television more

   ^{10}call us to remind us ^{11}don't call us to remind us

J.Stumphauzer 3-31-82

SUMMARY

This chapter reviewed the rationale for social skills training with delinquents and presented one such program in depth. Delinquent youth may be skillful at manipulating others, lying, bullying, and being aggressive. They may, however, lack such social skills as getting a job, keeping a job, problem-solving, and being assertive (standing up for their own rights *without* taking away the rights of others).

Discussion, modeling, role-playing, positive reinforcement, and shaping are all used to teach social skills and several programs were noted in this chapter. Results in general were found to be encouraging.

One such program was developed by the author and was presented in detail. Designed to teach teenagers on probation "how to stay out of trouble," the program is limited to ten weekly meetings. Each session, with its own topic, was outlined: (a) how to get off probation, (b) looking for a job, (c) job application and interview, (d) keeping a job, (e) problem-solving, (f) assertion vs. aggression, (g) assertion with authorities, (h) saying "no" to peer pressure to do crime, (i) being assertive in saying "no" to peer pressure to use drugs, and (j) social skills for getting through school. A detailed session-by-session "manual" and forms used in each session were included for further application and evaluation.

Four scales for behavioral assessment were presented to assess social skills, assertion/aggression, violation of minor rules and regulations, and consumer evaluation of the program by each youth. Preliminary results were noted.

The next chapter reviews the application of the social learning approach to probation. Such probation contracting clarifies the requirements of probation and the consequences for adhering to or violating particular requirements.

READINGS

1. Cartledge, G., & Milburn, J. F. (Eds.) (1980). *Teaching social skills to children: Innovative approaches*. New York: Pergamon Press.

    2. LeCroy, C. W. (Ed.) (1983). *Social skills training for children and youth.* New York: The Haworth Press.
    3. Ollendick, T. H., & Hersen, M. (1979). Social skills training for delinquents. *Behavior Research and Therapy, 17,* 547–554.

CHAPTER 8

Probation Programs:
Contracting to Stay Out of Trouble

Probation has been called "the greatest contribution of American criminal justice." Today, as many as three-fourths of all court convictions result in probation. Carney (1977) suggests five reasons for the popularity of probation:

1. The community is more normalizing than institutions,
2. it minimizes psychological and physical degradation,
3. it humanizes rehabilitation,
4. it is more effective than incarceration, and
5. it costs less.

Probation today, however, faces many serious problems. Over the years probation has become top-heavy with paperwork having little direct utility. In addition, probation has developed many traditions of understanding and handling casework that either simply don't work (i.e., don't change behavior) or are so inconsistent in their procedures that they cannot be evaluated.

Another serious problem today has been substantial cutback in funding for probation work resulting in incapacitatingly large caseloads, less stress on the counseling aspects of probation work, and an overall demoralizing effect on probation departments. Some of these departments have responded by overloading officers, developing a "hook and book" philosophy ("your job is to document probation violations and to bust the violators"), and downgrading positions—requiring minimal education and training so that probation officers can be paid less.

If one was to look at the traditional probation process with an eye to discovering its adequacy as an effective and humane social learning program, the result would be dismaying to say the least. Offenders are assigned to a "probation investigator" who gathers information and writes a time-consuming "probation report." Very few of the methods outlined in the chapter on assessment (Chapter Three) are utilized. Recommendations are vague ("psychotherapy is indicated") and, at that, do not logically follow from the data gathered. It appears as though some of these recommendations are stock phrases.

The youth is then assigned to a supervision officer who has the report and the youth in front of him or her. The officer often starts his own assessment (if they have the time). Finally, the youth is advised what to do and what not to do. These requirements are most often in the form of loose, vague, negative contingencies ("Stay away from bad influences . . . or else," "Obey your parents . . . or else," "No problems at school . . . or else," and "Keep your nose clean").

Most youths that I have interviewed over the years do not know what their probation means, exactly what is required for them to do or not do, and what will happen (consequences) if they do this or that behavior. In fact, the goal of the first of ten social skills sessions presented in Chapter Seven is to specify and clarify probation requirements and current assessment of status on each. However, typically the young people are faced with "trial and error" learning. That is, they will have to act first and then find out the consequences (if there are any). For example, a boy or girl might "cut" school and the probation officer may not find out about this truancy for several months and may or may not do anything about it.

The traditional probation officer uses one behavioral principle— one that does change behavior (temporarily) if applied systematically, but that has severe side effects. This principle is punishment or (the even more nebulous) threat of punishment. As you saw in Chapter Four, punishment is the *least* effective, the most problematic, and yet the most popular way to try and change behavior.

Before turning to a review of social learning approaches to probation, and then to some particular methods, let us look at a point by point comparison of traditional probation and behavioral probation methods for dealing with five major activities of officers: record keeping, plans for work with client, structure of contact with client, accountability, and incentives. This comparison, found in Table 26, was developed by Polakow and Doctor (1974a). It

Table 26

COMPARISON OF PROBATION AND BEHAVIORAL PROBATION

INSTITUTIONAL ACTIVITY	PROBATION METHOD	BEHAVIORAL METHOD
Record Keeping	Enter descriptive information about client, what he says about what he is doing.	Definition and Charting of target behavior. Identify goals in behvioral terms. Enter objective information as well as impressions about the client. Objective sources of information would involve proof of activities, visits to client in natural environment, visits or calls to significant others in environment. Changes in behavior would be monitored.
Plans for work with client	Develop generalized non-behavioral goals that have good social value such as reduce acting-out behavior, improve self-image, and ability to get along with others.	Develop organized sequential plan to work with client. Define your goals in objective behavioral terms and secondary steps toward goals. Behavioral plan as an educational function.
Structure of contact with client	Be open, responsive, inactive listener. The client is responsible for making self-corrections, you provide warm atmosphere and reflection.	Consequation rules are clearly defined as well as behavioral expectations within each sequential step. Client controls reinforcements. Behavior outside of office is reinforced irrespective of relationship with probation office.

TABLE 26 (Continued)

Accountability	Report psychological status of client on how hard you are working with him. Try not to get pinned down to specifics. Focus on terminal goals and deficits.	Keep accurate records of target behaviors. Base-line and continual recording provide evidence and speed of change.
Incentives	Use aversive control via threats, punishment by incarceration, fines, or continued probation if behavioral demands are not met.	Use of natural reinforcers in the system such as time off probation. Sequence behavioral expectations; show probability of successfull responses.

underscores major differences and suggests the superiority of behavioral probation.

SOME EXAMPLES OF BEHAVIORAL PROBATION AND CONTRACTING

In their classic book, *Behavior Modification in the Natural Environment,* Tharp and Wetzel (1969) were among the first to apply psychological learning principles to delinquent youths. They introduced a triadic model in which they saw the role of experts as consultants to mediators in the natural environment rather than as "therapist treating patient." They stressed that natural mediators such as parents and teachers were really in the best position to change delinquent behavior directly because they are a part of the youth's real, day-to-day life. Their model, reproduced below, was used with success directly in the community.

CONSULTANT→MEDIATOR→YOUTH

In their article on "new tools for probation officers," these authors saw probation officers as "having the potential for becoming experts in behavior modification." They noted that behavioral programs should *not* take more time because the cases discussed in their program were all seen for three sessions or less. They concluded that "the real change, though, would be that aversive methods would no longer be their only source of control. They could also be skilled in teaching parents how to put powerful positive rewards on contingency" (Thorne, Tharp, & Wetzel, 1967, p. 27).

Robert L. Polakow developed a remarkable "Behavioral Research and Training Program" within the Los Angeles County Probation Department which the author has discussed in some detail elsewhere (Stumphauzer, 1981b). Polakow and Doctor (1974a) describe their experience with bureaucratic resistance in probation and their attempt to change things from the inside. Polakow, a probation officer with a behavioral psychology background, stressed the following elements:

1. documenting behavior,
2. use of learning principles,
3. focus on court orders and client needs,
4. time off probation as a reinforcement, and
5. redefinition of probation activities (see Table 26).

Perhaps most remarkable, Polakow's program convinced the court to accept the plan of probationers earning time off probation in exchange for specified behaviors. For example, "ten days off probation for each job interview" rather than the more usual and vague "you've been doing pretty good; keep it up until your probation is up in six months."

In an extended case study, Polakow and Peabody (1975) reported a successful behavior probation program for a twenty-eight year old woman. This is a suggested reading because the focus on child abuse is especially timely today. This mother's behavioral probation contract stipulated not only a provision for improving her parenting behavior (using positive reinforcement with her son rather than punishment), but also included one week off probation for every week the program was adhered to.

A small number of studies have focused on the training of juvenile probation officers in behavior modification principles and methods. Diebert and Golden (1973) trained officers in six three-hour sessions and found important changes in knowledge, perceived competence, and in attitudes. In our training program (Burkhart, Behles, & Stumphauzer, 1976), we added a comparison group of officers who were not trained and a measure of competence: officers' ability to do behavioral analyses and behavioral probation plans. Trained officers (in the program outlined later) gained a significant degree of skill in these areas.

In a third training program Wood, Green, and Bry (1982) carried out an education program similar to the two above, but added measures of behavior change in the youths seen by the officers trained. Again, the probation officers did learn from such training and changes in the behavior of youths were found as well.

There is some question in these studies, however, whether probation officers trained in these skills will continue to use them or not—especially if their supervisors are not supportive of these new methods and if behavioral probation is viewed as "more work." In a six month follow-up Stumphauzer, Candelora, and Venema (1976) found that trained probation officers still demonstrated knowledge of the concepts but were not, for the most part, utilizing them directly in their work. There were exceptions: they reported increased use of positive reinforcement and use of principles of learning in their own lives (e.g., weight control and child rearing).

In part as a response to cut-backs in the Los Angeles County Probation Department and consequent curtailments of counseling functions, the social skills training program—"How to Stay Out of Trouble"—was developed in our mental health clinic. Youths on probation attend the ten sessions of social skills training completely outlined in Chapter Seven. In these sessions they are taught how to get off probation, how to get and keep a job, problem solving skills, assertion rather than aggression, and how to deal with pressure from friends to commit delinquent acts.

APPLICATION OF BEHAVIORAL PROBATION AND CONTRACTING

A. A Training Program for Probation Officers

Burkhart, Behles, and Stumphauzer (1976) trained probation officers from a juvenile division in six 2-hour, weekly workshops. Each of the six workshops consisted of an hour didactic presentation on the particular topic and the second hour was used for more direct learning of the new methods. This second hour included discussion of application to current cases, modeled use of the techniques, and problem solving. The course was divided into four major sections:

1. general principles of behavior modification,
2. behavioral assessment,
3. techniques of intervention, and
4. generalization to the natural environment.

A model probation officer who utilized these methods (in fact, Robert L. Polakow) was a guest instructor at the first meeting. As part of their homework, all officers participating in the program were given a programmed training manual (Stumphauzer, 1977), in which they completed eleven of the twenty-two basic chapters, including the following, which are noted here so that probation trainers can develop similar programs:

Ch. 1. Introduction
Ch. 2. Principle of Behavioral Analysis
Ch. 3. Principle of Behavior Measurement
Ch. 4. Principle of Positive Reinforcement
Ch. 6. Principle of Shaping
Ch. 8. Principle of Social Reinforcement
Ch. 9. Principle of Generalization
Ch. 12. Principle of Punishment: Aversive Stimulation
Ch. 15. Principle of Extinction
Ch. 19. Principle of Modeling and Imitation
Ch. 20. Principle of Self-Control

As further homework, all officers receiving the training did a behavioral analysis (see Chapter Three) and developed a behavioral intervention plan for one of their current clients. Finally, this program was incorporated as part of this probation department's in-service training; certificates of completion and credits toward promotion were given to those completing the program.

A related training program was carried out by Stumphauzer, Candelora, and Venema (1975), but this time with probation investigators. Since their major activity was evaluation and assessment of new cases, the goal was to teach them behavioral assessment skills (Chapter Three), and for them to incorporate this approach and information gained into their formal Probation Reports. A checklist for a social learning approach for the six fairly standard parts of the Probation Report was developed and utilized in training. The following are a few sample questions from the checklist used from each section of the Probation Report:

1. *Personal History:* Are behaviors specified in any manner, such as how often they occur, where, when, or with whom? Are non-problematic, good behaviors discussed?
2. *Use of Drugs and Intoxicants:* Are models for drug use discussed? Are reinforcements for drug use discussed?
3. *Present Offence:* Is the situation which led up to the crime specified? Are reinforcers for the present crime specified?
4. *Defendant's Statement:* Are behaviors discussed (rather than feelings and attitudes)? Is behavior presented as being learned?
5. *Interested Parties:* Are modeling relationships specified? Are interested parties discussed as potential mediators for improving behavior?
6. *Reasons for Recommendation, and Recommendation:* Is learning of behavior mentioned as the basis of the recommendation? Are contingencies (behaviors and their resulting reinforcements or punishments) recommended? If probation is recommended, is behavior necessary to get *off* probation specified?

B. Two Forms Used in Behavioral Probation

Robert L. Polakow developed two forms for use in the Los Angeles County Probation Department's Research and Training Program. The first was a "Reinforcement Survey Schedule for Probation" (a list of items such as "beer" and "watching TV" which adult probationers were to check with regard to how much pleasure each gives them from "very much" to "not at all"). The "Favorite Things" reinforcement survey presented in Chapter Three can be used in the same way with children and adolescents. With such reinforcement survey forms, a probation officer can determine what reinforcers or incentives are particularly important for each probationer. If practical (available, ethical, and controllable), these strong incentives—often unique for each person—can be utilized as reinforcement for behavior improvement by the probation officer or (more likely) by a mediator in the real day-to-day world: parent, teacher, friend. Alternatively, the youth on probation may reward him or herself in a program utilizing self-control (see Chapter Ten).

The second form developed by Polakow was a "Reinforcement Card." On it the probation officer can give "credit" for behavior improvement. This card was frequently used for giving time off probation as a reinforcement for productive behavior, behavior imcompatible with probation violation. For example, "Pay to . . . John Smith . . . two weeks off probation for two completed job interviews." The card would be signed and dated by the probation officer. These simple, printed 3 × 5 cards, a relatively immediate reinforcer, help bridge the gap until the actual but somewhat delayed reinforcement—getting off probation early—occurs some weeks or months down the line. Such cards could be adopted, with court cooperation, in any probation department. As noted before, this method of using time off probation was supported finally by this court and probation department: an exemplary, cost-effective use of social learning principles.

C. Probation Contracts

Typically, formal probation is not a behavioral or contingency contract. If I am to believe most of the youths I ask "What does your probation mean?" probation is a vague status that means "I have been caught, I am in trouble, I better not get in any more trouble (or, at least, I better not get caught?)."

In contrast, a behavioral probation contract is a formal agreement that specifies consequences (rewards and punishments) for specific behaviors. With this formal agreement there is a definite means for changing the behavior that got the youth in trouble. Many of the points covered in Chapter Six on behavioral family contracting also apply here. Therefore, six ingredients of behavioral probation contracting would be:

1. date contract begins,
2. a general contract,
3. specified responsibilities (productive, noncriminal behavior),
4. specified privileges (e.g., getting off probation),
5. a plan for measurement or assessment, and
6. signatures of those agreeing.

In Table 27 there is an actual "Agreement" drawn up by a probation officer for a 16 year old boy on probation. It is fine as far as it goes, but it is not a complete behavioral contract. It does contain three of the points listed above: date, responsibilities, and signatures. But it does not include three other key ingredients thatwould make it a more complete contract based on social learning principles: a general agreement, contingent privileges, and a plan for measurement.

The author has re-written this agreement in a form that would utilize all six parts of a behavior probation contract in Table 28. In this reformulated behavioral probation contract, the contingencies are made explicit, a means of measurement is instituted, responsibility for behavior change is explicitly specified and shared by the boy, his parents, and the probation officer.

Table 27

PROBATION AGREEMENT

AGREEMENT   March 15, 1985

1. Progress Report from Griffith Jr. High on/or before
   March 25, 1982

2. U.S.C. Medical Center, Children's Psychiatric Program,
   Appt. # 226-5302

3. At home schedule:
   a. Weekdays nights -- In by 10 PM, No exceptions
   b. Weekends -- in by midnight unless a very special occasion

4. Set-up volunteer work at Maravilla Center
   40 hours volunteer community services

_____   _____
      Parent   Court Counselor

_____
      Parent

_____
      Minor

Table 28

date **March 15, 1985**

B E H A V I O R A L   C O N T R A C T

PRIVILEGES	RESPONSIBILITES
GENERAL CONTRACT: In order to for Michael to get off probation...	we agree to ...**work on this program together.**

SPECIFIC CONTRACTS:

1. In order to **get off probation by July 1, 1985**	1. **Michael** and his parents agree to get a progress eport from Griffith Jr. High by March 25
2. In order to **help Michael stay out of trouble**	2. **Michael** and his parents agree to make an appointment at USC Med Center within two weeks.
3. In order to **stay out until midnight on weekend nights**	3. **Michael** agrees to be in by 10PM on weekday nights.
4. In order to **get off probation by July 1, 1985**	4. **Michael** agrees to do 40 hours volunteer services at Maravilla Center by June 1.

Bonuses and Sanctions: If Michael gets off probation by July 1, 1985 his parents agree to let him visit his brother in Texas this Summer. If he fails to do this by July 1, he will not be permitted to use the car for two months.
Who will measure what: Michael will sign in the time when he gets home each night; parents will keep records of school attendance, clinic attendance, and will get a report of hours served from the Maravilla Center.

SIGNATURES:

_____   _____
                                        Michael

_____   _____
Court Counselor   Parent

                               _____
                                        Parent

SUMMARY

Probation, "the greatest contribution of American criminal justice," often fails. In this chapter probation training programs and probation contracting, the application of social learning to this field, were reviewed.

Probation and the social learning approach are compatible: both stress intervention and prevention of further problems directly in the natural environment by natural mediators. However, traditional probation appears to be bogged-down in paperwork, bureaucracy, and ineffective technique (vague threat of punishment). "Keep your nose out of trouble or else . . . " simply does not help delinquents change.

The author and others have trained probation officers to apply social learning techniques. Two forms used in another program (reinforcement survey schedule and reinforcement card) were discussed. They have been used successfully for assessing reinforcers and for reinforcing probationers directly in court with "time off probation."

The concept of contracting (similar to that of family contracting) has been extended to probation. In effect, the conditions of probation are spelled out as are specific punishments (arrest, etc.)and reinforcers (time off probation, etc.). A sample agreement and its "fine tuning" by the author were presented.

Social learning approaches have been applied in many schools. Such school programming to help delinquents change is reviewed in the next chapter.

READINGS

1. Burkhart, B. R., Behles, M. W., & Stumphauzer, J. S. (1976). Training juvenile probation officers in behavior modification: Knowledge, attitude change, or behavioral competence? *Behavior Therapy, 7,* 47–53.

2. Polakow, R. L., & Peabody, D. L. (1975). Behavioral treatment of child abuse. *International Journal of Offender Therapy and Comparative Criminology, 19,* 100–103.

3. Wood, G., Green, L., & Bry, B. H. (1982). The impact of behavioral training upon the knowledge and effectiveness of juvenile probation officers and volunteers. *Journal of Community Psychology, 10,* 133–141.

CHAPTER 9

School Programs:
Staying in School and Learning
to Learn

All delinquents are of school age. This not-so-profound fact suggests that, obviously, schools may play a major role in delinquent behavior and in helping delinquents change. Indeed, much of what we call delinquent behavior occurs in and around schools—from truancy to theft, vandalism, illicit drug use, and violence. There have been many social learning programs that have dealt with changing or preventing delinquent behavior at school, and these programs are the topic of this chapter. There has been a full range of such programs from those developed for classrooms inside institutions for delinquents to those in regular neighborhood schools.

Over the last twenty years schools and educational programs have adopted a great many of the social learning approaches described in this book—for any number of academic problems, behavior problems, and, to a lesser degree, for delinquent behavior. Behavior modification and social learning principles are routinely included in the education of teachers, and these methods have become accepted practices in virtually all school systems. Special education classes in particular are often based upon behavior modification principles.

A great many books, manuals, and journal articles are devoted to behavior modification in schools. Two recommended texts are those of O'Leary and O'Leary (1972) and Walker and Shea (1980). The *Journal of Applied Behavior Analysis* often has articles dealing with school programming. This topic is the major focus of both *Behavioral Disorders* and *The Directive Teacher*.

Perhaps we should differentiate between delinquents who go to school and delinquent behavior in the school. Many delinquents go to school, but do not do any of their delinquent behavior (i.e., juvenile crime) *in* the school. For them there may not be a need for any specialized program in the school. However, a great many of these young people do have serious academic problems or learning disabilities. In fact, many theorists have suggested that learning disabilities, of whatever variety, cause delinquency. Many of the techniques dealing with academic problems in the texts and journals mentioned above would be appropriate in setting up programs for delinquents who have problems learning.

Delinquent behavior in and around schools is, perhaps, a different matter. Today, we continually hear about increased violence in schools, about teenagers and children carrying weapons to school, and about drug abuse on school campuses. This seems especially true in larger urban centers. School security has not only become a major concern for schools, but security is now taking a large part of the school budget. Amazing as it sounds, the second largest police force (ranking just under the LAPD) in California is the security police in Los Angeles City schools! There are airport-type security gates along with drug and weapon checks at the door. Many teachers have left the system out of fear. We may conclude that delinquent behavior in school is a major problem.

In comparison to the scope of the problem, few social learning programs have been reported which deal directly with delinquent behavior in and around schools. This chapter will survey some of these programs, will cover a few projects that have focused on the academic behavior improvement of delinquents, and finally will describe some actual techniques of school programming to help delinquents change.

SOME EXAMPLES OF SCHOOL PROGRAMS FOR DELINQUENTS

Many school programs have been developed for youths inside institutions for delinquents. In fact, these were some of the very first applications of learning principles to delinquents. They were described in some detail in Chapter Five, and that information should be reviewed.

Academic behavior, as well as delinquent behavior, has been a major focus in group homes as well (see Chapter Twelve). One particular such program warrants discussion here. Achievement

Place, the "grandfather" of behavioral group homes, has always stressed school success. Bailey, Wolf, and Phillips (1970) quite clearly demonstrated that the behavior of predelinquents in the classroom could be modified *from* the group home.

The boys required to live in the group home by the court or other social agency did attend regular community schools. Therefore, the "teaching parents" faced the problem all parents have—how to know what the boys were doing in school and how to help change behavior in the school if there were problems. Report cards are not very good measures of anything, and they are a delayed report at that. Schools do contact parents, even "teaching parents," after there is a "big" problem. It may be too late to do anything about it ("She's been getting in a lot of fights") and leave the parent with seemingly one alternative, since they must decrease the behavior: punishment. The many pitfalls and shortcomings of punishment were discussed in Chapter Four.

Bailey, Wolf, and Phillips (1970) circumvented virtually all of these problems quite simply and directly. The boys were already earning points in the token economy of Achievement Place. Now they were required to carry a 4 × 5 inch "daily report card" (similar to the Daily Behavior Card found in Chapter Three) back and forth to school every day, and they would earn points at *home* based on their *school* behavior. On the card the teacher was simply required to check a "yes" or "no" for "obeyed the classroom rules" and "studied the whole period." In short, the "teaching parents" were able to know what the boys were doing in school every day, they were able to reinforce good behavior, and they were able to change behavior in school from the home.

In 1975 President Gerald Ford signed Public Law 94-142. It mandates, in part, that a free, appropriate public education be provided for all handicapped children. It requires that formal Individualized Education Program (IEP) conferences be held, that parents be directly involved in these IEPs, and that each plan be formally written to spell out exactly what steps would be taken to meet each child's individual needs. IEPs and behavior modification are quite compatible as Walker and Shea (1980) have pointed out— behaviors are specified as are plans and dates to reach each goal. When delinquents fit the necessary classification (e.g., "emotionally handicapped"), then a concrete plan for their academic and delinquent behaviors will be developed and parents will be involved directly as well. IEPs may become a highly useful adjunct for changing the behavior of delinquents in school. The reader, if working with a particular delinquent youth, may be called in to attend such an IEP conference. At this point some of the programs outlined in this book could be offered as suggested parts of the IEP.

Filipczak, Friedman, and Reese (1979) report an ambitious project called PREP (Preparation through Responsive Educational Programs) whose goal was to *prevent* juvenile problems in public schools with four basic elements:

1. individualized programming for math and English for referred or volunteer students,
2. group interpersonal skills classes,
3. a behavioral educational program for parents, and
4. teacher/staff training.

Significant goals were reached with regard to academic tests, grades in PREP classes, discipline, and school attendance (the last two of which are highly relevant to delinquent behavior). In addition, improvement also generalized to other classes in which these students participated.

Three major delinquent behaviors in school will be discussed in more detail: stealing, aggression, and truancy. Then, more specific techniques will be described.

1. *Stealing* or theft is a common delinquent behavior in school. As noted several times in this book, stealing is very difficult to measure (especially if successful!), but its measurement and change have been reported (Stumphauzer, 1976b). In that case three sources all measured the stealing of a twelve year old girl: her teacher, her parents, and she self-measured as well. These records agreed and we proceeded to stop her stealing at school (and at home and in stores) with a combination of behavioral family contracting and self-reinforcement. There was no further report of stealing at school (previously a daily event) during 18 months of follow-up.

2. *Aggression* (fighting, anger, vandalism, etc.) is also a very common set of delinquent behaviors in school. There have been reports of changing such behaviors. In Chapter Ten, the author described a technique of self-control training where the focus was self-measurement of fights. Once the boy self-measured (with his diary and then card) and self-evaluated in counseling sessions, we were then able to explore what set off fights in school and how he could change these things.

Also in Chapter Ten, a procedure for Anger Control Training was described, and it has been used successfully directly in a school program. The three phases of training are: (a) education on how to view their own anger, (b) instruction and rehearsal of skills to cope with stress that had led to anger, and (c) application of this training to everyday life.

3. *Truancy*, tardiness, leaving school grounds, and "school phobia" have all received attention in the social learning literature. Why would a child or teenager not go to school, or be late, or cut school once there? The behavioral assessment is particularly important here. What is reinforcing their staying at home or in the neighborhood? Is something (e.g., failure) or someone (e.g., teacher or peer) being avoided at school? What are the positive consequences (if any) for going *to* school? What are the consequences for truancy? Two social learning techniques for changing truancy will be described in the next section.

APPLICATIONS OF SCHOOL PROGRAMMING
WITH DELINQUENTS

A. Ways to Decrease Truancy and Absenteeism

Schloss, Kane, and Miller (1981) developed a series of three questionnaires which pursue just such a line of query as that mentioned above (behavioral assessment of truancy). The three forms were designed for the parents of the youth, the truant boy or girl, and the teacher. The following are sample questions from each questionnaire:

1. *Parent:* What does your child do when he or she stays home from school? Does he or she have difficulty waking up in the morning? Are you willing to participate in a program to increase your child's school attendance?
2. *Student:* What do you do when you stay home from school? Do you enjoy those activities? What do you dislike about school?
3. *Teacher:* Does there seem to be a pattern to days in which the student does not attend school? What specific activities does he or she enjoy in school? What does the student dislike about school?

After completing this three part behavioral analysis, the authors report using the information to systematically decrease truancy. Intervention programs included (a) *in*creasing the satisfaction gained from going to school, (b) *de*creasing the gains for staying home, and (c) teaching social skills which increase the benefits of going *to* school.

A second set of procedures has been developed by Fiordaliso, Lordeman, Filipczak, and Friedman (1976). Their focus was absenteeism in junior high school students. The most common response of schools to absenteeism is to report this to parents by telephone or by mail. This is often a delayed report. Attention is being given to the negative behavior, often setting up the probability of punishment. This group changed this usual chain of events, and decreased absenteeism, through the use of positive phone calls and letters when truant students *did* attend school. Thus, they made more immediate response and were able to shift focus to the positive behavior (attending school) and to increase the likelihood of positive reinforcement with the use of "good news" phone calls and letters. This is a dramatic change in school-parent interaction, and is far different from "Oh no, a letter from the school . . . *now* what have you done?"

B. Behavioral Contracting in Schools

Behavioral contracts, or contingency contracts as they are some-times called, are a formalized series of exchanges. In this case they are exchanges between teachers and students, and they specify exactly what the student is to do and what they will receive in exchange for doing the specified behavior. The general technique has been described in detail in Chapter Six (behavioral family contracting) and in Chapter Eight (probation contracting).

There have been many successful applications of behavioral contracting between teachers and nondelinquent students with regard to academic behavior. This general approach has been used for academic behavior in institutions for delinquents (Chapter Five) and in group homes (Chapter Twelve).

Walker and Shea (1980) describe contingency contracts as they can be used in regular community schools. One of their sample contracts deals with a delinquent behavior: fighting. The contract was dated, included the name of the student and teacher, began and ended on specified dates, and was signed by both. The terms of the agreement were that if the student "did not engage in any fights during the school day for the period of the contract" then the teacher would "take the child to a Golden Gloves boxing match at the local arena." Some might object to the use of "going to a boxing match" as a reinforcer even though boxing is legal and not the same as "street fighting." More socially desirable reinforcers might be selected. Obviously, such school behavioral contracts could include parents and others (e.g., probation officer) as well.

C. Parent Training for Changing Behavior in School

Parent training and parent education are integral parts of successful school programming, and this may be especially true for parents of delinquents. It is probably obvious throughout this book that parents play a major role in delinquent behavior and, therefore, in helping delinquents change. There is a greater likelihood of changing the academic and delinquent behaviors in school if parents are actively involved—whether it is in IEPs, contingency contracting, or involvement in a comprehensive parent education program.

Walker and Shea (1980) have a excellent chapter on training parents in home-school behavior management and a step-by-step outline for such a program. Its objectives are (a) to train parents in the understanding and application of social learning principles, (b) to assist parents in changing selected target behaviors in their children, and (c) increased parent-school cooperation. The series of eight one-and-a-half-hour sessions they outline in detail are:

Lesson 1. An introduction to behavior modification.
Lesson 2. Consequences of behavior.
Lesson 3. Selecting potentially effective reinforcers.
Lesson 4. Strategies to increase behavior.
Lesson 5. Strategies to increase behavior, continued.
Lesson 6. Strategies to decrease behavior.
Lesson 7. Strategies to decrease behavior, continued.
Lesson 8. Ethical and effective application.

D. School Consultation and Preventing Vandalism

School vandalism continues to take too large a share of school budgets at a time when these funds are facing general cuts.

Therefore, any cost-effective method to reduce vandalism should be given serious consideration. Vandalism or purposeful destruction or damaging of school property (from graffiti to breaking windows and fire-setting) are serious delinquent behaviors.

Mayer, Butterworth, Nafpaktitis, and Sulzer-Azaroff (1983) have reported a remarkable three year program in eighteen schools to prevent vandalism and improve discipline. A team of consultants went to a series of schools and presented training workshops and consultation sepcifically with regard to vandalism. The development of classroom, schoolwide, and neighborhood programs that would *teach students alternative behavior to vandalism* was stressed as was reinforcement (praise) for such alternative behavior. Students were engaged in such nondelinquent or even anti-vandalism behaviors as "playground management." The cooperation of neighbors was enlisted during "neighborhood walks," and there was discussion in the schools and communities of how to use money saved from reduced destruction of school property. Vandalism was reduced an average of 78.5% for all project schools. This group's ten-point social learning approach to school consultation may well be useful in other school programs to help delinquents change:

1. establish a professional working relationship and develop communication skills,
2. identify behaviors of concern and roles,
3. start contingency analysis during interview,
4. observe behaviors in classroom situation,
5. confer with teachers; discuss what has been tried,
6. jointly develop treatment strategy,
7. develop and apply strategies to facilitate treatment utilizing a variety of reinforcing sources,
8. observe and record frequency of target behaviors,
9. develop and apply strategies to facilitate maintenance, and
10. share results!

E. Skill Streaming in Schools

Some would make a case for not including social skills training as a regular part of school curricula, that it doesn't fit with traditional education of reading, writing, and arithmetic. Stephens (1981) has made a strong argument for including social skills instruction in school, and, indeed there are many reports of such work including Stephens' own. He suggests that the basic social institutions (family, church, etc.) are undergoing great changes and are no longer doing an adequate job of preparing young people for life in society. He concludes that teaching information alone (traditional subjects) is not enough.

Goldstein, Sprafkin, Gershaw, and Klein (1980) have developed a detailed program for adolescents they call "Skill Streaming." They provide not only a manual for conducting such groups in schools, but also three audio cassette tapes with samples of their application with real high school students. While the program is not directed toward delinquents in school as such, many of the topics covered are quite pertinent for such youths.

For example, there are sessions on how to deal with accusations, responding to failure, making a complaint, and keeping out of fights (just to list a few). In their manual, Goldstein et al. provide "skill cards" which are given to each adolescent to use with homework assignments. The top half of the skill card asks five questions which are filled out by each student during the class training session: (a) what skill will you use, (b) what are the steps for the skill, (c) where will you try the skill, (d) with whom will you try the skill, and (e) when will you try the skill? The bottom half of the card consists of four questions to be filled out by each student *after* doing assigned homework applying that skill from that training session: (a) what happened when you did the homework, (b) which steps did you really follow, (c) how good a job did you do in using the skill (excellent, good, fair, poor), and (d) what do you think should be your next homework assignment? Although not yet reported, Skill Streaming (and the closely related social skills training of Chapter Seven) would appear to have direct relevance for helping delinquents change in school.

SUMMARY

The fact that all delinquents are of school age is no revelation. The ineffectiveness of most schools to help delinquents change is less well known. Several social learning approaches to delinquents in school have shown promise, and they are reviewed in this chapter.

For twenty years social learning and reinforcement programs have been utilized directly in schools—both for academic achievement and for behavior problems. It was a natural extension to focus on the behavior of delinquents as well: truancy, aggression, theft, vandalism, and academic underachievement.

In one such application, the behavior of problem youths was modified in school by use of a "daily report card" which was consequated each day back in a group home called "Achievement Place." Federally mandated IEPs (individualized educational programs) were presented as fully compatible with social learning approaches.

Programs to prevent delinquent behavior in school, behavioral analysis of absenteeism and truancy control, behavioral contracting in schools, parent training for changing behavior in school, vandalism reduction, behavioral school consultation, and Skill Streaming in schools were all reviewed.

Many delinquents are referred directly to therapists or counselors. Clinical behavior therapy, approaches to help delinquents change through one-on-one counseling in the office, is presented in the next chapter.

READINGS

1. Mayer, G. R., Butterworth, T., Nafpaktitis, M., & Sulzer-Azaroff, B. (1983). Preventing school vandalism and improving discipline: A three-year study. *Journal of Applied Behavior Analysis, 16*, 355–369.

2. Schloss, P. J., Kane, M. S., & Miller, S. (1981). Truancy intervention with behavior disordered adolescents. *Behavioral Disorders, 6*, 175–179.

3. Walker, J. E., & Shea, T. M. (1980). *Behavior modification: A practical approach for educators.* (second ed.) St. Louis: C. V. Mosby Company.

CHAPTER 10

Clinical Behavior Therapy: Office-Based Approaches

A great many delinquents are referred to clinics, mental health centers, and private psychotherapists (psychologists, psychiatrists, social workers). Still others are seen by probation officers, school counselors, and clergy. Many of the behavior therapy or social learning techniques described in this book were developed in clinics and offices by highly trained professional psychotherapists. Together these facts suggest specialized behavior therapy for helping delinquents change is readily available from professionals in clinics or offices (what I call clinical behavior therapy). This may or may not be the case.

Some psychotherapists are highly trained in behavior therapy—first in their university courses and then in direct supervised work with clients. Indeed, some universities and training programs have specialized in social learning and behavior therapy as have selected internships and psychiatric residency programs. As a rule, psychologists today have behavior therapy a part of their education and training, and this is also true for psychiatric social workers. For psychiatrists this is generally less so, although it depends upon the training program.

At this moment there is no "certification" for behavior therapy and many people call themselves behavior therapists. The Association for the Advancement of Behavior Therapy (AABT) does have a directory of members, although membership does not imply any particular qualifications. The Behavior Therapy and Research Society has a "roster of clinical fellows" which is published annually in the *Journal of Behavior Therapy and Experimental Psychiatry*, but again, this is no guarantee of expertise.

If you are referring a youth and his or her family to a professional therapist specifically for clinical behavior therapy, you should inquire about qualifications and experience in this area. Also, it should be pointed out that there are fewer professional behavior therapists who have experience working with adolescents than there are who routinely work with adults and younger children. There are fewer still with training and experience in clinical behavior therapy with delinquents.

Two of the clinical behavior therapies that a professional would utilize in his or her office are described in detail elsewhere in this book: behavioral family contracting (Chapter Six), and social skills training (Chapter Seven), and they will not be described here again, although they might be frequently applied clinical behavior therapy techniques.

The professional behavior therapist in this area usually does not work in isolation and does not expect that a one-hour-a-week visit is going to be enough to help a delinquent change. Therefore, clinical behavior therapy is often done in conjunction with still other methods covered in this book. The therapist might also be consulting with the youth's probation officer on a probation contracting program (Chapter Eight). Delinquents are often having severe problems in school, and school programming (Chapter Nine) may well be called for. The professional, clinical behavior therapist may, in addition, attempt to intervene directly in the youth's community (Chapter Thirteen), or help them do something incompatible with crime such as get a job (Chapter Eleven).

It may begin to sound as though a clinical behavior therapist, when faced with treating a delinquent in his or her office, would consider virtually all the chapters of this book. That is indeed the case and is the reason this book grew from experience and research into a treatment manual to assist those interested in selecting and applying approaches to help delinquents change.

How does the behavior therapist choose among these possibilities and determine where to begin? The answer to this question is found in Chapter Three: one conducts a behavioral analysis of the delinquent, his or her immediate environment, and of the resources available and pertinent to each case. The treatment choices, therefore, are logical choices that should become evident once the behavior analysis is complete, when the therapist reviews his own expertise or that of other possible mediators (e.g., teacher, probation officer), and finally decisions are made when the family agrees to proceed with treatment or counseling—to help delinquents change.

Over the years a number of clinical behavior therapy techniques have evolved (some quite recently) and are being utilized to change delinquent behavior from the office or clinic. Some are highly technical; some are not. Some have legal and ethical issues associated with them (such as whether one can use painful stimuli to change behavior), and therefore their use may be restricted or prohibited. Examples of these clinical behavior therapies will be given below, and then some more detailed applications will be presented.

SOME EXAMPLES OF CLINICAL BEHAVIOR THERAPY WITH DELINQUENTS

Six clinical behavior therapies will be described and note will be made regarding their particular application with delinquents seen in clinic offices. For the most part, they are highly technical and require substantial training.

1. Cognitive Behavior Therapy

In recent years there has been a trend toward a more mediational breed of clinical behavior therapy exemplified in the work of Bandura (1969, 1977), Mahoney (1974, 1977, 1979), and Meichenbaum (1977). For example, one focus has been on "self-speech," i.e., what clients say to themselves. It may be that delinquents say the wrong things to themselves, such as "I have no choice . . . there's no way I'll ever earn a bike like this . . . I can't wait, anyway . . . so I'm going to steal it . . . and I'm smart enough not to get caught . . . " Sound familiar?

The behavior therapist would try to assess what these thoughts and "beliefs" are (perhaps by getting clients to "think out loud" or to write down their thoughts). The therapist would assess the stimuli and consequences of these thoughts, help the delinquent clients understand the sequence of events that gets them in trouble, and finally teach more adaptive self-speech leading to more adaptive behavior—to nondelinquent behavior.

Camp (1976) showed that aggressive boys fail to utilize verbal mediation in achieving control over their own aggression. Then

Camp, Blom, Herbert, and vanDoornick (1977) developed a cognitive behavior therapy called (aptly enough) "Think Aloud," which taught cognitive self-control of aggression to children. Unfortunately, to my knowledge this promising approach has yet to be applied directly with aggressive delinquents.

2. Self-Control Training

A clinical behavior therapy closely related to the previous one is self-control training, and it is highly relevant to helping delinquents change. Controlling their own behavior, to stay out of trouble and to live more productive lives, is a skill many delinquents need to learn. It can be taught. Kanfer and Karoly (1972) have described three stages for self-control or self-regulation training:

a. self-monitoring,
b. self-evaluation, and
c. self-reinforcement.

The first stage is self-monitoring or self-recording. In this stage the client is taught to measure or count their own behavior, and is reinforced for doing so (e.g., counting "number of fights" per day on a Daily Behavior Card). In the second stage, self-evaluation, the youth is taught literally to evaluate the results of their self-monitoring, and to compare it to what they ought to be doing. How many times did they fight this week? Is there a *pattern* to their fights, such as they usually occur after school? What sets off and what reinforces them? Finally, in the third stage the client learns self-reinforcement (and perhaps self-punishment). They learn to praise themselves. For example, "I did really great talking my way out of that fight!" For a detailed example, the reader is referred to McCullough, Huntsinger, and Nay (1977) who present a case study on the self-control treatment of aggression in a sixteen year old boy.

The author utilized self-control training as part of the clinical behavior therapy of stealing (Stumphauzer, 1976b). The twelve year old girl self-monitored stealing, she learned to self-evaluate the circumstances of her stealing and what to do instead. Then she was taught to praise herself for not stealing—first aloud and then to herself (cognitive behavior therapy).

3. Aversion Therapy

Aversion therapy is a very controversial, highly technical clinical behavior therapy. It is controversial because it requires the use of painful stimuli (usually mild electric shock to the forearm). It requires sophisticated apparatus and a high level of technical expertise.

In aversion therapy, or aversive conditioning as it is sometimes called, cues or images that had been associated with the particular deviant behavior (e.g., photographic slides of the kind of woman that the criminal had raped) are repeatedly paired (given together) with the painful shock. Theoretically, with enough pairings conditioning will take place, and the deviant behavior will decrease as an "aversion" to those particular cues develops. Aversion therapy has been used with such problems as drug and alcohol abuse as well as sexual deviations. Less has been done with criminal behavior.

Only one case has been reported utilizing aversion therapy with a delinquent: an adolescent exhibitionist in England who exposed himself to older women (MacCulloch, Williams, & Birtles, 1971). The treatment was successful, and it was reported that at follow-up the boy had an "age-appropriate" girl friend.

In the 1970s, many ethical and legal issues were raised about the use of aversion therapy, especially without "informed consent," and this clinical behavior therapy is rarely used today and is mentioned here because of its historical importance and theoretical link to the next technique. Aversion therapy *is* used in combination with other treatments in some smoking control or weight control clinics. However, clinical behavior therapies utilizing mainly positive stimuli (positive reinforcement and modeling) are most often used, are effective, and they are less controversial.

4. Cognitive Sensitization

But what if one could carry out aversion therapy using *thoughts* of painful stimuli (e.g., thinking of extreme, painful nausea) rather than real painful stimuli? Such a clinical behavior therapy has been developed by Cautela (1967) and called cognitive sensitization. Cautela did report using this approach successfully with delinquents and with drug abuse problems. To give the flavor (pardon the pun) of one such office treatment session with an adolescent car thief, the following scene is quoted below (Cautela, 1967, p. 462):

> You are walking down a street. You notice a real sharp sports car. You walk toward it with the idea of stealing it. As you're walking toward it you start to get a funny feeling in your stomach and you have a slight pain in your gut. As you keep walking, you really start to feel sick, and food starts to coming up in your mouth. You're just about to reach for the handle of the door and you can't hold it any longer. You vomit all over your hand, the car door, the upholstery inside, all over your clothes. The smell starts to get to you and you keep puking from it. It's all over the place. It's dripping from your mouth. You turn around and run away and then you start to feel better . . .

While Cautela reports success with a few delinquents (stealing, glue sniffing), cognitive sensitization has yet to be adequately evaluated as a clinical behavior therapy with delinquents. Also, Kanfer (1977) notes that this treatment requires careful preparation of the client and that the client be highly motivated to change—often not the case with delinquents.

5. *Problem-Solving*

As Little and Kendall (1979) suggest, many adolescents are in trouble because they don't know what steps to take to problem-solve; they don't know how to cope effectively in social situations. Spivack, Platt, and Shure (1976) have developed what they call interpersonal cognitive problem-solving skills (ICPS) which included teaching the following to adolescents: means-end thinking, alternative thinking, and perspective taking (i.e., role taking).

D'Zurilla and Goldfried (1971) have presented five stages of problem-solving that could be central to clinical behavior therapy with a delinquent:

    a. general orientation or ''set,''
    b. problem definition and formulation,
    c. generation of alternatives,
    d. decision making, and
    e. verification.

In fact these five steps form the problem-solving segment of the group social skills training program for youths on probation described in Chapter Seven. Once these steps are taught in the group they are used again and again whenever a problem or topic warrants it (e.g., "finding a job," "getting out of a neighborhood gang"). A therapist might well teach these steps to an individual client or incorporate problem-solving into a comprehensive clinical behavior therapy in helping delinquents change.

6. Stress-Inoculation and Anger Control Training

Meichenbaum (1977) developed a clinical behavior therapy he called stress-inoculation which involves three phases for the control, in this instance, of anxiety and stress:

a. educational phase (provide client understanding of the nature of his or her particular response to stressful events after a behavioral assessment),
b. rehearsal phase (provide client with a number of skills to cope with stress), and
c. application training (once client has practiced coping techniques, this behavior has been shaped and reinforced in the office, and finally the client tests the coping skills by actually using them in their real-life stressful situations).

Stress inoculation could be a clinical behavior therapy for an individual delinquent whose reaction to stress had been getting him or her into trouble. However, stress inoculation has instead been extended by Novaco (1975) into dealing with a reaction to stress that is very pertinent to the treatment of many delinquents—anger. Anger control training follows the three phases above, but in this particular instance includes: (a) education on how to view their own anger, (b) instruction and rehearsal of skills to cope with stress that had led to anger, and (c) application of this anger control training to everyday stress. Stress inoculation training for adolescent anger problems is reviewed by Feindler and Fremouw (1983). They present conceptual discussion, review, a case-study, and a group treatment program.

Obviously some of these clinical behavior therapies are related to each other and to other topics in this book. Some authors might call self-control training, cognitive sensitization, and anger control training all forms of cognitive behavior therapy. Here they have been made separate but related topics.

As noted earlier, it is not likely that one such therapy would be used by itself; rather, other adjuncts are often incorporated. Examples of this might be individual behavioral contracts between therapist and delinquent, perhaps the use of tangible reinforcers or "points" to increase compliance with treatment or clinic attendance, and various other techniques for changing delinquent behavior described in this book. We will now turn to some more specific case applications of clinical behavior therapy.

APPLICATION OF CLINICAL BEHAVIOR THERAPY WITH DELINQUENTS

Some of the actual methods of clinical behavior therapy were described in the previous section. More on specific methods can be learned on each by consulting the readings and references given. However, clinical training and supervision may be required before the reader actually applies them in helping delinquents change. The techniques below, with some real case examples, will give the reader some samples of day-to-day clinical behavior therapy.

1. Self-Control Training: Self-Monitoring of Fights

A common problem for many delinquents is getting into fights. This often leads to problems in school, at home, and at times with contact with the law. However, fights do not usually occur in front of the therapist or counselor. Sometimes they do! Most often, however, such delinquent behaviors are not easily observed. As noted in Chapter Three, such behaviors are difficult or impossible to measure with traditional methods. It may well be desirable to help the youth to measure his or her own behavior (self-monitoring). Also, as you have seen, this is the first step in self-control training.

Problem behaviors such as fighting are perhaps best approached from a comprehensive clinical behavior therapy which would include self-monitoring. It would be necessary, however, to obtain the youth's cooperation in order to do this, and the following clinical example begins at that point.

Alan was a twelve year old boy who was referred to our clinic by his school because he "had a bad temper, was constantly fighting, and was often sent home after fights." A comprehensive clinical behavior therapy included the shaping of his self-evaluation so that *he* would observe what he was doing and, with help, *change his own behavior*. We began with getting Alan to keep a daily "journal" or diary and to make note about the events of any fights. This was a new behavior for him. In order to minimize resistance and to get his cooperation to do this, the following behavioral contract was negotiated and signed:

I have agreed to keep my journal for a week and to bring it in on Tuesday.

Alan

We agree to give Alan the checker set from the toy supply if he brings his journal in for every day of the week.

Therapist

This gave us the opportunity to discuss the week's events in some detail, and to evaluate the circumstances of fights: when they occurred, what in particular set them off, and what the consequences were (both immediate and long-term.) This kind of journal also allows the therapist to note positive, good behaviors, and to reinforce them. The following is an actual sample from Alan's journal—the chain of events is especially clear in this sample:

WEDNESDAY

Morning I ironed clothes for school. Went to school and ate breakfast at school. Then bell rang, went to my safety job, after that reading, then recess, then math, then lunch, thats when I had a fight with a kid. I bumped into him accidently, and he started to do karate judo on me and he kicks me, so I clip him in the eye and I did not get in trouble and that was the end of Wednesday.

A final example of self-monitoring in this case was a switch from use of a daily journal to use of a Daily Behavior Card (Stumphauzer, 1974b; see sample in Chapter Three). A journal or diary may be sufficient for on-going self-monitoring, but it is a running narrative and may not entirely meet the needs of the assessment for clinical behavior therapy. In this case we wanted to switch our attention to incompatible behaviors (*not* getting into fights vs. fights and to going *to* school rather than truancy). The Daily Behavior Card lends itself particularly well for this, and adolescents will carry them. The four behaviors used on Alan's Daily Behavior Card were:

a. not getting in fights,
b. number of fights,
c. went to school, and
d. cut school.

This approach to self-control training did help reduce fighting in this boy. The journal and Daily Behavior Card helped him self-monitor and self-assess (we were able to count fights; together to discuss the pattern, stimuli, and reinforcers); and then to switch to reinforcement for instances of *not* fighting: praise, some tangible rewards, and self-reinforcement.

2. Problem-Solving: Getting a General Equivalency Diploma (G.E.D.)

Teaching problem-solving skills is especially important in clinical behavior therapy with delinquents because it is a general approach that may be used with any new problem that they may face. It is a skill to be used throughout life. Adolescents often express the feelings that "It's not up to me" and "I have no choice." These beliefs are addressed directly in the first steps of problem-solving training (general orientation, beliefs, or "set"). This is followed with a step-by-step plan that answers the youth's questions about "what do I do now?" The following case example will illustrate.

Rick was a seventeen year old youth with a long history of delinquency, substance abuse ("I was an alcoholic"), and gang involvement ("I am the oldest member of the Little Cobras"). He initially came to my attention when he voluntarily came to the Social Skills Training group described in Chapter Seven as a "guest" of another client. Rick was to remain on probation for another two years for theft.

He joined the group voluntarily, quickly picked up the skills, practically became a co-leader of the sessions, and expressed interest in becoming a counselor. However, this goal seemed impossible—he had dropped out of high school in the 10th grade, he had no job, and he didn't know exactly how to get "from here to there.'' He needed to solve the long range problem of ''how to become a counselor or psychologist.''

In Table 29 there is the seven point plan for problem-solving that was developed with him as a way to solve this and other problems. The form is used in one of the Social Skills Training group sessions. Here the blanks were filled in by Rick with regard to reaching his goal. It was stressed that *he* was the one in control of this, and that he *did* have choices. Note the three choices that he now thought faced him. The results of each choice, both short and long term, were discussed.

Doing nothing or starting and dropping out of school again would be ''easy'' for the moment, but he would not be satisfied. As he put it, ''I'm not a kid anymore,'' and, ''My family would think I'm a bum.'' The short term results of going back to school would be ''It

Table 29

PROBLEM-SOLVING

1. You can handle it. You have control.
2. you DO have choices.
3. What are your choices? You always have at least three!

   a. Keep doing what you always do:"start back to school

      and then I quit."

   b. Do nothing.

   c. Do something different:"Go back to school and

      finish the G.E.D."

4. What are the results of each choice for you and

   for others?

   "For a. and b. my family will think I'm a bum."

   "For c. I would get what I want and they would be proud."

5. So what is your plan?

   a. Overall goal: "to be a counselor or psychologist."

   b. Plan on how to do it is: "get G.E.D., then Jr. College."

   c.The first step is: "enroll in Monrovia Adult School tomorrow."

6. Now, DO IT !

7. Did it work?   If so, great!   If not, now what?

wouldn't be easy to keep going to school'' and "It takes money."
But he could verbalize that the long range results were what he
wanted: "to be a counselor," "to help my homeboys," and "to
have a good job."

The next step, "Your Plan," got Rick down to specifics: he had
to actually write down his "overall goal," thus making a more
public commitment. His particular plan involved first getting a
G.E.D. (General Equivalency Diploma) and then going to junior
college. But those plans were still pretty far off in the future and
may have looked too unattainable and discouraging. Therefore,
what was stressed was for Rick to determine for himself what was
the very first step in all this—what can be done TODAY. In his case
it was enrolling in the G.E.D. course at the local adult school. That
was something he *could* do that day.

"Now, DO IT!" as step number 6 told him. He *did* it. Finally,
in step 7 there is self-evaluation in the form of "did it work?" and
"how is it going?" He is now attending the special class on Monday
nights, and as he said recently, "so far, so good—I'm doing it." He
has also graduated from the social skills group, became a volunteer
in the Los Angeles County Department of Mental Health, and
became a volunteer assistant counselor in that group!

3. Teaching Self-Reinforcement: "I'm Doing Good, I'm Proud"

The case of a twelve year old girl who was treated for frequent
stealing behavior has been discussed elsewhere in this book
(Stumphauzer, 1976b). As part of that clinical behavior therapy
(also involving behavioral family contracting, self-monitoring, and
bibliotherapy for her parents: reading behavioral child rearing
books), she was taught to self-reinforce.

Following the example of Meichenbaum's (1977) work in teaching children first to think out loud, and then to themselves, we
focused the individual treatment in the office on learning *self-
reinforcement for NOT stealing*. For example, she was taught the
following self-statements which she practiced out loud in the office,
and then practiced saying them to herself in the office.

    a. "I'm doing good,"
    b. "My parents will be pleased with me," and
    c. "I'm proud of myself for not stealing anymore"

At first the girl found this uncomfortable, but these statements were modeled for her by the therapist, and then she was given praise for repeating them. Gradually, they became easier for her and compliance increased.

Finally, she was instructed to self-reinforce during the week when she first turned away from looking at something she might steal (e.g., money from a purse on the playground), and also when she recorded zeros on her Daily Behavior Card for *not* having stolen anything that day. Stealing ceased within a few days and did not reoccur during one and a half years of follow-up. This girl took a active role in changing her own delinquent behavior. The clinical behavior therapy helped her change.

SUMMARY

A great many delinquents are referred to clinics, mental health centers, and private psychotherapists. In this chapter various social learning and counseling approaches utilized by professional psychotherapists in one-to-one clinical behavior therapy were reviewed.

Some of the techniques already presented in previous chapters have equal application directly in the therapy office: behavioral analysis, family contracting, and social skills training. In addition, a number of other office-based clinical behavior therapy techniques have evolved and are being utilized to help delinquents change.

In cognitive behavior therapy, beliefs and self-statements are approached from a social learning perspective. In self-control training, a three stage approach is the focus: self-monitoring (quantitative), self-evaluation (qualitative), and self-reinforcement. Aversion therapy, rarely applied because of its controversial use of painful/noxious stimuli, pairs antisocial behavior with mild electric shock or other painful stimuli to build an "aversion" to criminal behavior. A related approach called "cognitive sensitization" circumvented that controversy by pairing criminal behavior repeatedly with *imagined* pain or nausea. Problem-solving teaches general strategies for step-by-step coping with any problem situation. Finally, stress-inoculation and anger control training were reviewed as potentially applicable to youth whose reaction to stress or anger gets them in trouble. Three cases from the author's clinical practice were used as examples of applications of three of the above approaches.

In the next chapter the social learning approaches to occupational skills training is presented in conjunction with the general belief that jobs help change or prevent delinquent behavior.

READINGS

1. Feindler, E. L., & Fremouw, W. J. (1983). Stress inoculation training for adolescent anger problems. In D. Meichenbaum, & M. E. Jaremko (Eds.) *Stress reduction and prevention.* New York: Plenum Press, 451–485.

2. McCullough, J. P., Huntsinger, G. M., & Nay, W. R. (1977). Self-control treatment of aggression in a 16-year-old male. *Journal of Consulting and Clinical Psychology, 45,* 322–331.

3. Stumphauzer, J. S. (1976b). Elimination of stealing by self-reinforcement of alternative behavior and family contracting. *Journal of Behavior Therapy and Experimental Psychiatry, 7,* 265–268.

CHAPTER 11

Occupational Skills Training: Finding a Job and Learning to Work

A major aspect of changing delinquent behavior is the teaching or building of behaviors that are incompatible with crime. One important class of such behaviors is working or employment. It is generally believed that young people who have jobs do not get in trouble and, conversely, that unemployed youths are more likely to commit delinquent acts. Fleisher's (1966) sociological data do indicate a relationship between unemployment and delinquency. Today, with unemployment (especially youth unemployment) on the increase, there is special reason for concern. Will increased youth unemployment result in increased delinquency? Furthermore, budgets have been cut for the very programs that promised to change this trend: job training and employment programs and even summer jobs for youth.

Can job skills be taught? Can employment skills be learned by adolescents who have been in trouble? If they learned these skills would they find jobs, keep jobs and stay out trouble? For discussion here, job skills can be divided into two general categories: (a) the general social skills having to do with employment, and (b) the specific work skills necessary for the particular job. Let an example clarify. We will use a major, omnipresent youth employer for our example: McDonald's fast food restaurants. The general social skills with regard to this employment might be: locating the job, asking for an application, filling out the application, responding to a job interview, negotiating hours and wages, being on time, appearance (clean and neat), keeping the job (by being reliable, responding to superiors etc.), and perhaps advancing in the organization (assistant manager, manager, Ronald McDonald, etc.). In addition, there are particular work skills to be learned such as taking customers orders, operating a cash register, making change, and all those skills to prepare the food so that "Big Macs" and "Quarter Pounders" are not "Big Pounders" and "Quarter Macs."

SOME EXAMPLES OF OCCUPATIONAL SKILLS TRAINING

The two topics—delinquency and employment—each, separately, have large and complex literatures. However, in combination (i.e., the link between delinquency and employment) the research literature is quite limited. There are chiefly two sides of the coin that will be reviewed here. The first is that unemployment causes or, at least, is highly correlated with delinquency. The second is that, *as an intervention,* providing a job program for delinquents (perhaps in combination with other treatments) will *reduce* delinquency.

Evidence that links unemployment and delinquency is, for the most part, sociological in nature. Fleisher (1966), in a fairly comprehensive study, found that youths who were not employed were more likely to be arrested than were youths who had jobs. While the data are correlational and provide no direct causal proof, they are strongly suggestive of such a link. Also, these findings support a "common sense" view that many would like to believe. However, some recent research suggests that employed youth may have problems of their own, and that employment in young people may have "costs" that have been ignored. Greenberger and Steinberg (1981) studied suburban 10th and 11th graders who were holding their first job. In this sample no evidence was found that employment necessarily deters delinquency, that as many as 60 percent reported stealing on the job or "giving away" goods or services, and that those working 15 hours or more per week spent *less* time on school work and school activities than did their unemployed peers. Elsewhere, however, the same authors suggest another *positive* effect of youth employment: an understanding of work and less egocentrism—less of a belief that the world revolves around them (Steinberg, Greenberger, Jacobi & Garduque, 1981).

But what about programs that have focused on an employment program as a *treatment* for delinquents? Does employment change delinquent behavior? Shore and Massimo (1979) describe a vocationally-oriented psychotherapeutic program for delinquent boys not only noteworthy for its comprehensiveness, but even more remarkable for their follow-up reports two, five, ten, and even fifteen years later! In their initial report, Massimo and Shore (1963) report a thorough, ten-month program for delinquents that included intensive psychotherapy, remedial education, and job placement for ten delinquents who were compared to ten nontreated, randomly assigned delinquents. Unfortunately, the authors gave little description of actual procedures (especially job placement) and relied on ''soft'' psychological test results and mental constructs, but they did report changes in behavior. Treated boys were arrested less, did better in school, and had a far superior job record. Perhaps even more important, these differences held up over the two, five, ten and fifteen years of follow-up (Shore & Massimo, 1979). With such limited numbers treated, and such promising results, the authors did call for a much needed full-scale replication of their program.

Many delinquent youths have difficulty reading and filling out job application forms and, thus, are stopped in pursuing a job even before they begin. This very topic— completing job applications— was the focus of a suggested reading by Heward, McCormick, and Joynes (1980). They first completed an item analysis of the application forms of 30 employers in their area and then formulated a ''Master Employment Application'' which contains 35 typical items requiring biographic information. This or any ''standard'' application may be useful in first assessing a youth's ability to fill out such a form then in training them to do so. For the Social Skills Training program described in Chapter Seven the author went in to the nearest McDonald's restaurant and asked the manager for their application form. Heward, McCormick and Joynes divided their application into four sets of items and proceeded to teach them, set by set, to a group of mildly retarded delinquents in an institution through use of ''points'' as positive reinforcements. Not only did this group, who would usually have difficulty, learn to complete this ''Master Employment Application'' correctly, but this new skill generalized to three real job applications as well. Such behavior *can* be taught and learned.

The Kentfields Rehabilitation Program in Grand Rapids, Michigan included youth employment as an integral part of its comprehensive program (Davidson & Robinson, 1975). The goal was to provide a community-based alternative to incarceration for virtually *all* adjudicated youths in this community—including, most remarkably, relatively "hard core" delinquents (repeat, serious offenders). The comprehensive program included keeping the youths in their own homes, *public works participation each morning for wages,* an afternoon school program based on programmed instruction, as well as performance contracts, behavioral group sessions twice a week, and an overall point system. Admirable indeed! Results were most encouraging with reduction of delinquent behavior, increases in prosocial performance, and (especially noteworthy today) a significant reduction in costs over usual institutionalization. The youths were picked up by bus five mornings a week; they received a basic wage for a variety of public work programs for three hours a day: tree trimming for local parks, litter removal for the department of highways, working on playgrounds for the schools, painting for the YMCA, and building renovation for local community projects. This program should provide a good model for other cities: a cost-effective program more humane than incarceration.

In Chapter Seven a ten session social skills training program for adolescents on probation was presented which included three sessions on occupational skills training. The first of these three sessions ("finding a job") included self-assessment (abilities, personal characteristics, experience), looking for a job (newspaper, agency, or asking a relative or friend) and practice in filling out a real job application form obtained from that frequent youth employer, McDonald's. In the second session, ("practice job interviews") each youth was interviewed on videotape and their behavior shaped utilizing modeling, feedback, and positive reinforcement (praise and attention). Finally, in the third session, "how to keep a job" was taught by stressing what employers look for: reliability, willingness to learn, and handling potential on-the-job problems. While this program is still under evaluation, the employment skills sessions do appear highly relevant, highly rated by the probationers, and useful. A related program, but designed for jobless adults, is the "Job Finding Club," a suggested reading (Azrin, Flores, & Kaplan, 1975). It included some components potentially useful for delinquents: group meetings, a "buddy" system for helping each other, family support, and the sharing of job leads. Within two months 90 percent of those in the "Job Club" were employed. We will now explore in detail a behavioral employment program for delinquents.

APPLICATIONS: A BEHAVIORAL EMPLOYMENT PROGRAM FOR DELINQUENTS

Mills and Walter (1979) developed a remarkable, social learning program for shaping employment in delinquents. More complete details are given in that reading. The program not only taught the youths "how to work" but had a major effect on their delinquent behavior as well. Youths who completed the program were also arrested less, institutionalized less, and remained in school longer than a comparison group who were not taught how to work. Perhaps one reason for the success of this program was that *the employers' behavior* was shaped as well. All too often the youths are the only focus and they may or may not meet with success in the "real world." They might make one mistake on a new job and be fired. The general procedure and forms utilized follow.

The youths were court referred and were relatively serious offenders (arson, armed robbery, etc.). Employers in the local community were recruited and apparently motived in that (a) they had jobs to fill, (b) they were willing to help shape "good working habits" in new employees, (c) the authors would help with employee problems, and (d) they were reimbursed for 50 percent of the youth's wages for the first three months of employment. Specifically, the procedure for the employers was the following:

1. Employers gave the teenager's paycheck to experimenter.
2. Employers filled out weekly feedback sheets describing the subject's performance which were given to the experimenter and discussed with the youth.
3. Starting pay was at least $1.50 per hour.
4. Youths received, as a minimum raise, $.20 per hour at the end of Phase I and II.
5. Each day employers asked for and initialed youth's checklist. (see Table 31.)
6. Employers met weekly with experimenter to discuss the subject's progress.
7. Employers terminated a teenager who did not meet his or her obligations to the experimenter.
8. Employers signed a contract agreeing to the above.

Employers' behavior was shaped during weekly meetings with

the researchers: praise was used whenever employers said positive things about the youths and the employers were ignored if they said general, negative things about "delinquents."

Shaping was also used by Mills and Walter with each youth. In an initial interview with the youth, all positive statements about desire for working or getting jobs were positively reinforced with praise, head nods, etc. A behavioral contract similar to the following was also signed during the first session:

CONTRACT

1. I agree to see the experimenter once a week during Phase I and biweekly during Phase II.
2. I agree that the employer will give my paycheck to the experimenter and she will give it to me at the end of our weekly meeting.
3. To receive the paycheck I agree to bring in my report each week.

Signatures: Youth _____

Experimenter _____

When possible a delinquent was matched to job interest and location and was called in for an orientation and taken to the job interview. Advice on behavior and grooming was given, and a job interview was role-played. Each youth was asked to list eight behaviors they felt were important in keeping a job. Such "Employer Expectations" are given in Table 30. Also, the delinquents were asked to fill out the Checklist Sheet reproduced in Table 31 once a week during orientation, Phase I, and Phase II. Two points were given for each behavior listed and another point if the employer signed each as completed. Points were plotted on a graph youths could see in the author's office.

During Phase I (beginning employment) a high level of positive social reinforcement (praise, attention), in addition to the points, was given by the employers and authors for pro-job behaviors. Employers also completed the "Feedback" sheet found in Table 32 once a week listing for each youth "things did well" and "things could improve on," although the stress was on the positive side. During Phase I the seven following behaviors were the focus:

1. Being at work every scheduled day.

3. Being on time.
4. Calling in ahead of time if ill or if going to be late.
5. Following regulations of organization, including dress code, lunch time, and breaks.
6. Good job performance (specified behaviorally according to youth's job).
7. Learning names of employees with whom the subject was in contact.
8. Cooperation in following directions.

Table 30

EMPLOYER EXPECTATIONS

1. Be on time.

2. Be at work every scheduled day.

3. Do work expected for the job, thoroughly.

4. Dress according to employer guidelines.

5. Follow orders.

6. Cooperativeness.

7. Willingness to learn.

8. Friendliness with co-workers.

9. Friendliness with clients, custormers, tenants, etc.

10. Notify employer if going to be late or absent, well before scheduled time.

11. Take only time alloted for breaks, lunch, and only at times specified.

12. Do not use telephone during working hours.

13. Do not have friends, realatives stop in at work.

14. Interest in the organization and your part in it.

15. Get enough sleep to function well on the job.

16. No drugs or alcohol on the job, during breaks or lunch, or before work.

17. Honesty, no stealing or "borrowing" anything belonging to the the organization, no lying when you do not feel like working.

18. Little or no smoking on the job.

19. Accepting responsibility, looking for things that need to be done without having to be told, i.e., if work is finished, not sitting around.

20. Transportation to and from work planned for each day, ahead of time.

Table 31

CHECKLIST SHEET

Name_____
next appointment_____
week of_____

THINGS I WANT DO DO THIS WEEK ON MY JOB	M	T	W	T	F	S	S
_____							
_____							
_____							
_____							
_____							

EMPLOYER´S SIGNATURE

THINGS I NEED TO IMPROVE ON THIS WEEK
1.

2.

3.

4.

GOOD THINGS THAT HAPPENDED AT WORK THIS WEEK
1.

2.

3

4.

THINGS THAT HAPPENED AT WORK THAT I DID NOT LIKE THIS WEEK
1.

2.

3

4.

When youths earned a total of 240 points they graduated from Phase I and moved on to the next phase. In Phase II (maintaining employment) reinforcement, feedback, and meeting with the experimenter were all faded to less frequent occurence. Written feedback forms (Table 32) were no longer required; reports were verbal. Youths now completed a checklist once a week instead of once a day. The experimenter was seen every other week. Finally, in Phase II, to further shift to the ''natural'' rewards of employment, pay was increased. Phase II was completed when each youth earned another 300 points. At that time the experimenter requested by letter that the youth be released from the court's jurisdiction.

Phase III (fade program out) usually began about six months after starting the program and continued for another year. Contact with the experimenter was minimal (informal, about once a month). Intermittent (once in a while) social reinforcement was given to youths and employers for their progress. Mills and Walter report that results strongly support this "learning to work" program: 85 percent of youths in the program were judged "successful," 90 percent had no further arrests, and 86 percent remained in school as well. This social learning program for helping delinquents change by shaping employment skills is remarkable in its cost-effectiveness, humane approach to delinquents and certainly warrants that other communities try and assess these procedures. Shaping the behavior of *both* the delinquents *and* the employers at the same time seems especially promising.

SUMMARY

It is generally believed that young people who have jobs do not get in trouble and, conversely, that unemployed youths are more likely to commit delinquent acts. Today, youth unemployment and cuts in funding for youth employment are added concerns. The

Table 32

EMPLOYER'S FEEDBACK SHEET

EMPLOYEE_____   WEEK OF_____

THINGS DID WELL THIS WEEK	THINGS COULD IMPROVE THIS WEEK
1.	1.
2.	2.
3.	3.
4.	4.
5.	5
6.	6.
7.	7.
8.	8.

EMPLOYER_____

social learning approach to employment skills training for delinquents was covered in this chapter.

Some research has supported the belief that employment prevents delinquency. Other studies have found that employed youth do admit to minor delinquencies. One vocationally oriented psychotherapeutic program for delinquents reported long-term success in decreasing delinquent behavior. The social skills training program described in Chapter Seven included three sessions (out of ten) on job skills: locating a job, job application/interview, and keeping a job.

A program reported by Mills and Walter was presented in more depth. They not only taught delinquent youth "how to work," but shaped their employers' behavior as well. A behavioral "contract" between each youth and program staff was followed by a phase system: in Phase I a high level of praise/attention was given by employers and program staff; in Phase II reinforcement and feedback were gradually faded to a more natural, realistic level. When Phase II was complete the court was asked to release the constraints on each youth. Those who completed the program were arrested less, institutionalized less, and remained in school longer than a comparison group.

This chapter showed that employment skills can be taught to delinquent youth and that this remains a promising approach to delinquency treatment and prevention. The next chapter reviews social learning programs in neighborhood group homes. It will be shown that intervention can be effective directly in such community settings.

READINGS

1. Azrin, N. H., Flores, T., & Kaplan, S. (1975). Job finding club: A group-assisted program for obtaining employment. *Behavior Research and Therapy, 13,* 17–27.

2. Heward, W. L., McCormick, S. H., & Joynes, Y. (1980). Completing job applications: Evaluation of an instructional program for mildly retarded juvenile delinquents. *Behavioral Disorders, 5,* 223–234.

3. Mills, C. M., & Walter, T. L. (1979). Reducing juvenile delinquency: A behavioral-employment intervention program. In J. S. Stumphauzer (Ed.) *Progress in behavior therapy with delinquents.* Springfield, IL: Thomas.

CHAPTER 12

Group Treatment Homes:
Learning to Live in the Community

What reasonable, community based alternative is there to institutionalization for delinquents? There is a general belief, and considerable evidence, that "punishing" or "rehabilitating" or "correcting" juveniles by putting them in institutions does not improve their behavior. Institutionalization may indeed change behavior, but in the direction of *increasing delinquent behavior*!

President Lyndon Johnson's Commission on Law Enforcement and Criminal Administration concluded in 1967 that institutionalizing juvenile offenders did not result in effective rehabilitation, was expensive, and was even inhumane. In simple terms, it was cost-*IN*effective. That commission recommended community-based treatment programs as the most reasonable alternative.

LeCroy (1984) and Goocher (1984) review and discuss current trends in residential treatment services such as group treatment homes utilizing token economies, training child-care staff, encouraging parent involvement, and programming group activities in residential treatment. Another recent trend is the proliferation of private, short-term hospitals for the treatment of behavior problems and drug abuse in adolescents.

In the late 1960s, first attempts at establishment of group homes for juvenile offenders based on behavior modification were begun. There was a strong rationale for this development. If criminal and other social problem behaviors were to be changed or prevented, it would be most effective and more humane if these programs were carried out directly in the "real world," in a teaching-family setting, following social learning principles.

There was promise that such group homes might be more effective in the long run and cost less than institutions in the short run. Could they replace institutions with their extensive history established in juvenile justice, corrections, and general beliefs that criminals (even young criminals) should be locked up some distance from the general public, which needs to be protected? These programs are the focus of this chapter.

SOME EXAMPLES OF BEHAVIORAL GROUP TREATMENT HOMES

In the mid-1960s a group of psychologists at the University of Kansas began the first group home for young offenders based on behavioral psychology. The name they gave it, "Achievement Place," aptly stressed the positive approach based largely on gradual reinforcement and shaping of productive, prosocial behavior which was incompatible with delinquent behavior.

This home was a regular rented house in the community. The staff consisted of one set of "Teaching Parents" well trained in behavioral science. Eight boys, referred by the court or school system, lived in Achievement Place, and attended regular community schools. Over the years, this arrangement gave the developers and researchers at the University of Kansas's Department of Human Development the opportunity to develop and evaluate the various treatment elements of the program.

Achievement Place was first described in detail by Phillips (1968) who, incidentally, was (together with his wife) one of the first teaching parents. Broad areas of social, self-care, and academic behaviors were the general focus. Youths earned points in this home-style token economy for particular behaviors (e.g., homework) and lost points for other specified behaviors (e.g., arguing and stealing). Points that the boys earned could be traded in for privileges or "back-up reinforcers" such as allowance or permission to go downtown.

Allen, Phillips, Fixsen, and Wolf (1972) wrote a novel which gives a close account of one boy's experience in entering Achievement Place. In order to give a flavor of the actual day to day process of behavior change in Achievement Place, the following quote from that novel is given. This is a brief excerpt near the beginning, while the boy and his "new family" were finishing lunch on his first day. Especially make note of the behavior, contingency, social, and token reinforcement, the measurement, and importance of peer attention; the subtle application of behavioral principles in a home-like setting:

> I finished off the sandwich and chips in a hurry and got up. The wife was still eating, but she looked up at me, everybody else did too, like I did some terrible thing.
> "Would you please carry your dishes to the sink, Paul?"
> Man, oh man, I felt like telling her, I ain't no damn waitress, lady, but I kept quiet. I looked at the warden, and he nodded his head, meaning I had to do what she said. "But that's woman's work," I said louder than I planned.
> My voice sounded weird to me, cause I'd hardly said nothing out loud since I left the courthouse. All the guys looked around at each other, rolling their eyes and grinning, and I thought, these sons of bitches, ain't nobody going to laugh at me, you'll see.
> "We all do things here you'll probably call 'woman's work,'" the warden said. "Elaine couldn't possibly do everything for all of us, and there's no reason why she should. We want you to learn to do things for yourself while you're here. Now please carry your dishes to the sink."
> He said that all pretty nice, not grouchy or like he lost his temper. I took the damn dishes over to the sink, since I didn't figure that he'd let me out of there until I did.
> "Good, Paul, that's fine, thank you, give yourself 500 points."
> This guy was like a broken record. But I wrote down 500 points for "carrying dishes to sink," and the warden put a big "L" by it, but he erased the "S" and put "M" and said it was for maintenance or something. The guys were being quiet, watching again.

Phillips (1968) reported the systematic assessment and modification of five socially relevant behaviors in Achievement Place boys utilizing baseline designs and systematic positive reinforcement and fines. The behaviors modified were (a) aggressive statements, (b) bathroom cleaning, (c) punctuality, (d) homework, and (e) use of the slang word "ain't."

Subsequent research has focused on particular treatment elements of the program: self-government system (Fixsen, Phillips, & Wolf, 1973), a home-based report card system to change behavior in school (Bailey, Wolf & Philips, 1970), and a vocational training program (Braukman, Maloney, Fixsen, Phillips & Wolf, 1974). The use of peer-managers and self-government is an especially noteworthy trend. As Fixsen et al. (1973, p. 31) describe the program, it "is a semi-self-government system whereby the seven pre-delinquent youths can democratically establish many of their own rules of behavior, monitor their peers' behavior to detect violations of their rules, and conduct a 'trial' to determine the consequences for a youth who violates a rule."

More recently, the Achievement Place approach has spread through training teaching parents in a year long program at the University of Kansas and a national Teaching Family Association. Kirigin, Braukman, Atwater, and Wolf (1982) report six regional training sites and approximately 170 "Teaching Family" group homes throughout the United States. The Achievement Place model of a group home has been replicated by others (e.g., Liberman, Ferris, Salgado, & Salgado, 1975). In addition, the author is aware of attempts in England, Holland, and Mexico to extend the model program to other countries and cultures.

Major evaluations of the Achievement Place program (both of individual program components and general effectiveness) have been reported in recent years. Dramatic changes in behavior are demonstrated by various component evaluations while some lasting results, cost-effectiveness (costs ranging about one-third that of institutions!), and positive "consumer evaluations" by the boys themselves have been documented (Kirigin, Wolf, Braukman, Fixsen, and Phillips, 1979).

Michelson, Wood, and Flynn (1982) reported an independent, long-term follow-up of the Achievement Place program in Florida. They found, for example, a 13% recidivism rate for Achievement Place graduates compared to 69% for unsuccessful graduates. A more extensive evaluation has shown mixed results (Kirigin, Braukman, Atwater, & Wolf, 1982). The original Achievement Place programs were evaluated along with 12 replication homes and 9 comparison homes which were not utilizing these methods. The results during treatment were better for the Achievement Place homes. In the post-treatment year, however, no major differences in juvenile offences between programs were found.

While there were some design limitations to this study (absence of a no-treatment control group that might have done worse than these treatments and reliance on "official delinquency" as the measure of success), the lack of long-term, positive results suggests a failure to fulfill the promise of a completely effective community-based, home-style alternative for delinquents. Other evaluations are constantly underway in this large network of homes.

Are there other models of group homes based on social learning principles? Learning House, based in Palo Alto California and attached to Stanford University, provided one notable alternative model. It grew, in large part, out of Carl Thoresen's previous research experience in the area of behavioral self-control (Thoresen & Mahoney, 1974).

One could describe the Achievement Place model detailed above as a contingency management program based on positive reinforcement and shaping. In contrast, the Learning House model stressed self-control training in addition to reinforcement (Thoresen, Thoresen, Klein, Wilbur, Becker-Haven, & Haven, 1979). Furthermore, the Learning House program provided a full range of components aimed at maximal generalization to continuing success later, after the youths returned to their regular homes:

1. an initial point (positive reinforcement) phase,
2. behavioral-contracting,
3. self-rating,
4. behavioral parent counseling, and finally
5. continuing care after they return home.

Yates, Haven, and Thoresen (1979) introduced some new methods of cost-effectiveness research and used them to evaluate the initial success of Learning House. Two levels of cost-effectiveness were demonstrated:

1. *MACRO* cost-effectiveness (global outcome measures such as cost of nonrecidivism), and
2. *MICRO* cost-effectiveness (detailed breakdown of cost per behavior changed).

Together, Achievement Place and Learning House represent outstanding examples of humane, cost-effective group home application of social learning principles. They appear to be viable alternatives to reformatories and institutions. However, to my way of thinking, two types of key evaluations of these programs remain to be done. First, no one has reported utilizing the behavioral group home model with relatively "hard-core" delinquents. Rather, most of the work reported has been with "predelinquents" or offenders with mainly minor offenses. This must be demonstrated before these models can be offered as serious alternatives to institutions. Second, a juvenile court or community needs to be convinced to assign youths *randomly* to these behavioral group homes and to regular institutions. Only then will results be less equivocal and more far-reaching. We will now turn to some detailed applications of these group home techniques in the hope that they may be better understood, applied elsewhere, and further evaluated and refined.

APPLICATION OF GROUP HOME APPROACHES

A. Achievement Place

Phillips, Phillips, Fixsen, and Wolf (1974) have developed The *Teaching Family Handbook,* which is used both as a training manual for prospective, new teaching parents and as a manual for the routine running of individual homes. It provides fine points on the motivation (reward) system, self-government, management of social and school behaviors, house-care and self-care, homeward bound programming, steps for completing program evaluations, and various appendices.

Phillips (1968) gave a breakdown of behaviors in Achievement Place boys that earned points (positive reinforcement) or lost points (punishment in the form of response cost). The following are some examples of behaviors and points:

> BEHAVIORS THAT EARNED POINTS:
> watching news on TV: 300
> doing dishes: 500 to 1000
> performing homework: 500
>
> BEHAVIORS THAT LOST POINTS:
> speaking aggressively: 20 to 50
> being late: 10 per min.
> stealing, lying, or cheating: 10,000

Once points are earned, youths in Achievement Place can trade them in or spend them for a wide variety of privileges (back-up reinforcers) such as:

PRIVILEGES: PRICE IN POINTS
biycle: 1000
TV: 1000
snacks: 500
permission to go downtown: 1000

An especially noteworthy component of the Achievement Place program was the addition of methods to assess consumer satisfaction with the program. That is, to what degree were the boys themselves pleased with the various aspects of Achievement Place and how does this compare to consumer evaluations of other programs? See Chapter Seven for another example of consumer evaluation used in a social skills training program. The following is a sample question from the Achievement Place Youth Evaluation:

Are you satisfied with the fairness of the program in giving rewards and punishments, such as giving and taking away of privileges?
__ completely satisfied
__ satisfied
__ slightly satisfied
__ neither satisfied nor dissatisfied
__ slightly dissatisfied
__ dissatisfied
__ completely dissatisfied

B. *Learning House*

Learning House initially utilized a point system not unlike Achievement Place. Later, however, each child moved to a behavioral contracting phase which was more individualized and the youth had more of a negotiated say in his or her contract. These contracts are similar to the behavioral family contracts found in Chapter Six. In one such contract a boy agreed to reduce arguing in exchange for having a friend over for dinner.

The self-control training of Learning House consisted of a series of sessions which taught children (a) to increase commitment, (b) to develop awareness of the stimuli and consequences of their behavior, (c) to rearrange their particular environment (including their thoughts), and (d) to evaluate self-standards and to reinforce themselves for their own behavior change. A more detailed outline of the self-control training follows:

Commitment

1. Review reasons why self-control helpful.
2. Positive incentives to encourage the application of self-control skills.
3. Child perceiving himself as the "kind of person who can use self-control" through teaching another child the skills he has learned.
4. Review progress with peers and teaching parents during the family meeting.
5. List positive consequences of demonstrating self-control.

Awareness

1. Recognize target behaviors through role-playing and video-tape feedback.
2. Count target behaviors on wrist counters.
3. Rate daily performance on target behaviors and compare with teaching parents rating.

Rearranging the Environment

1. Cognitive: (a) self-instruction training, (b) problem-solving training.
2. Social: (a) teaching self-control skills to another child, (b) discussing progress with peers and adults.
3. Physical: (a) conspicuous display of charts indicating progress, (b) "cue" card and signs to remind oneself of daily goals, use of self-instruction.

Evaluation of Standards, Consequences

1. Set daily goals for target behavior (contracts).
2. Self-administer contingent consequences for completing contracts.
3. Use self-rating of daily performance to earn privileges.

Note the sequence and the broad range of social learning principles applied. This process of acquiring self-control is made more clear by the "self-control training homework" of Billy given in Figure 6.

When I want to, I really can do what I am asked and finish the whole job. Today, I was able to **pick up the checkers game and get all the pieces back in the box.**
When I do what I am asked and get the whole job done, I feel **happy!**
A problem that I may have tomorrow is **at recess on the school playground with a group of 5th grade kids bothering me.**
To help me solve this problem I will remember to say to myself:

1. **What is the problem? — Being "bugged" by kids at school.**

2. **What are my choices? — Call them names, Tell the teacher, fight, ignore.**

3. **Choose one — Ignore them.**

4. **Do it! — So, I'll ignore them.**

5. **Praise myself! — I feel terrific!**

Today, I counted a total of **7** cooperative responses, and I completed a total of **3** jobs without having to be reminded.
The Teaching Parents counted a total of **9** cooperative responses and **1** procrastination/off-tasks.
I have recorded this information on my self-correct graph in the dining room: **X** yes _____ no.

Signed **Billy**
Date **April 19**

FIGURE 6. Self-control training "homework" in Learning House.

Finally, both Achievement Place and Learning House have used "school notes" or "daily report cards" to change behavior in the school from the home. They are similar to the Daily Behavior Card (Stumphauzer, 1974b) presented in Chapter Three.

While any one of these behavioral group home techniques may improve an already functioning group home, it is their particular combination that will determine any such group home's success or cost-effectiveness:

1. the training of the teaching parents,
2. the systematic application of principles,
3. planned generalization to the child's regular home, and
4. careful evaluation and subsequent program change.

SUMMARY

What reasonable, community-based alternative is there to institutionalization of delinquents? In this chapter social learning approaches in group homes for delinquents were presented as one such alternative.

Institutionalization of delinquent youth is, to put it simply, cost-*IN*effective. Since the late 1960s behavioral group homes have provided models for intervention that are not only effective, but they cost less than institutions. Two such programs were reviewed in this chapter.

Achievement Place is a "home-style token economy" with trained "teaching parents" who utilize points and social reinforcement to shape behavior at the home and at the public school which the youths attend. For example, points might be earned for reading a newspaper, doing homework, or desirable grades and behavior on report cards. Or points could be lost for fighting, stealing, or failing grades. Accumulated points can then be "traded in" for privileges such as allowance, trips downtown, or permission to come home late after school. This model has been applied throughout the United States and has been implemented in other countries as well. Results are very encouraging but institutions and traditional probation remain the more popular choices by most courts.

A second program, Learning House, was described. This program stressed self-control training in addition to reinforcement and shaping through five phases: (a) initial point (positive reinforcement) phase, (b) behavioral contracting, (c) self-rating, (d) behavioral parent counseling, and (e) continuing care after release to their own homes.

Together, Achievement Place and Learning House represent outstanding examples of humane, cost-effective group home application of social learning approaches—viable alternatives to reformatories and institutions. However, studies using these methods with relatively "hard-core" delinquents or random assignment to a behavioral group home or institution remain to be done.

In the next, final chapter, broader community approaches to delinquency are reviewed. Can social learning principles be applied in understanding, changing, and preventing delinquent behavior in entire neighborhoods or communities?

READINGS

1. LeCroy, C. W. (1984). Residential treatment services: A review of some current trends. *Child Care Quarterly, 13*, 83–97.

2. Phillips, E. L., Phillips, E. A., Fixsen, D. L., & Wolf, M. M. (1974). *The teaching-family handbook.* Lawrence: University of Kansas Printing Service.

3. Thoresen, K. E., Thoresen, C. E., Klein, S. B., Wilbur, C. S., Becker-Haven, J. F., & Haven, W. G. (1979). Learning house: Helping troubled children and their parents change themselves. In J. S. Stumphauzer (Ed.) *Progress in behavior therapy with delinquents.* Springfield, IL: Thomas.

CHAPTER 13

Community Programs and Prevention: The Ultimate Answer?

Delinquent behavior does not usually occur in your office, in the home, or even in school. For the most part delinquency is learned in the community and it occurs in the community. Most of the stimuli and consequents that control delinquent behavior are in the neighborhood or community as well. Delinquent behavior occurs in city streets, in parks, in cars, in stores, after school, in the evening, and on weekends. Therefore, it would seem most logical if programs to help change or prevent delinquent behavior also took place in the community. By and large, this is *not* the case.

This chapter describes those programs that *have* tried to understand and change delinquent behavior in its natural environment— in the community. This is not a traditional corrections or traditional psychotherapy model, but is more closely aligned to a community mental health model. I hasten to add that it is not a traditional behavior therapy model either, except that finally we are heeding our own dictum that *ENVIRONMENT CONTROLS BEHAVIOR*, and are doing something *in* that environment. We can call the general approach in this chapter behavioral community psychology. Two books on this topic are recommended (Nietzel, Winett, MacDonald & Davidson, 1977; Glenwick & Jason, 1980). Feldman (1983) has reviewed the psychotherapeutic and behavioral approaches to prevention and intervention.

We have a history (in both corrections and in mental health) of having the person go to a place to be "corrected" or "treated" by an expert, official, doctor, or professional. The people in those systems, with all their structures like police stations, probation offices, juvenile halls, mental health clinics, and institutions for delinquents will take a long time to change their conceptualizations and practices. Currently, there is no such structure or plan to change or (even better) prevent delinquent behavior directly where it occurs. Instead we have developed very expensive and largely ineffective institutions and personnel practices to change delinquent behavior—often long after it has occurred—and almost no program or organization to prevent delinquent behavior. Today, with cutbacks and financial crunch at every turn, this seems even less likely to develop.

Many innovative people in the social learning or behavior modification field have been active in designing and developing programs directly in the community. Why? I believe the answers lie in behavioral analysis (Chapter Three). After completing behavior analyses of problems, including juvenile crime, it became apparent that the behavior is best understood and changed and prevented directly where it occurs. Several examples of such community programs will be described below. Then community behavioral analysis will be outlined. Finally, prevention of delinquent behavior will be discussed.

SOME EXAMPLES OF COMMUNITY PROGRAMS
AND PREVENTION

Social learning principles have been applied in a variety of ways to many aspects of life in the community. Some of them are covered in detail elsewhere in this book: in behavioral family contracting (Chapter Six), in probation contracting (Chapter Eight), in school programming (Chapter Nine), in clinical behavior therapy (Chapter Ten), in occupational skills training (Chapter Eleven), and in group treatment homes (Chapter Twelve). However, most of these programs are examples of helping delinquents change in fairly traditional settings. In this chapter the focus will be largely on unconventional, more direct ways to help delinquents change in the community.

One of the best examples of a social learning program for helping delinquents change directly in the community is perhaps the oldest as well. This is a series of projects carried out by C. W. Slack and his students Ralph and Robert Schwitzgebel. The work is summarized in a highly recommended book by Schwitzgebel (1964). They went directly to a high-crime neighborhood and rented a storefront as a base of operations. Next, they recruited delinquents right off the street to come in and talk into tape recorders. Gradually, they shaped the behavior of delinquents. It was many years before such direct methods for changing delinquent behavior were to become a focus.

Another whole area of community programming is behavioral community consultation. In these programs the expert in behavioral psychology goes directly to a community program or agency and provides consultation and assistance to those who will help behavior change in the community. One of the best examples of behavioral community consultation is the work of Todd Risley of the University of Kansas. He provided consultation directly to a housing project called Juniper Gardens (Risley, 1972).

Risley took an innovative step and began attending a monthly tenants' association meeting, listened to the community's concerns (delinquency, vandalism, litter, loud parties, etc.), and then offered his assistance as a consultant so that they could change the problems in their own community. Utilizing the psychological principles of learning, he helped them change their own neighborhood problems in a series of projects. This behavioral community consultation model is a far cry from sending one community member to an expert's office, a far cry from "doctor" treating "patient."

An area related to consultation is training. Those active in social learning approaches to problems in living have often recognized that they are not the major "changers of behavior," but it is the "natural mediators" discussed in Chapter Eight who must be reached. However, such natural mediators as parents, teachers, and neighbors may be lacking in the very knowledge and behavior-change skills that could be given to them through training.

In Chapter Eight, I described our behavioral training program for probation officers. Two colleagues and I also developed a similar training program for paraprofessional community workers (Teicher, Sinay, & Stumphauzer, 1976). These paraprofessionals were "people of the streets:" they had experienced some of the very same problems they were now helping with, and they currently lived and worked in central Los Angeles communities. They were all working with youth who had multiple problems from substance abuse to gang violence. In our training we taught them behavioral family contracting skills to work with families of alcohol abusing teenagers, and with some encouraging results. We passed on a skill to those directly involved in day-to-day life on the streets.

Volunteers are largely an untapped resource in this field. A major program in the state of Hawaii made use of volunteers as "buddies" in a behavioral community program (Fo & O'Donnell, 1974). Adult volunteers recruited through newspaper ads were trained in basic social learning principles and methods, and then were assigned to be the "buddy" for up to three delinquents at a time. Results were improvements in such things as school attendance and aggression, although later it was found that boys who did not have a record actually did worse after contact with the program. The utilization of volunteers is remarkably simple and promising approach—one that should cost very little—and it should be tried in other communities and evaluated further.

Another untapped community resource is senior citizens. There have been many reports on the gradual increase in the number of retired and senior citizens, the so-called "graying of America." It would be possible both to help young people and to improve the "quality of life" of volunteer senior citizens if the seniors could become helpers with delinquent youths in their neighborhoods. Some colleagues and I trained volunteer "Foster Grandparents" to rate videotapes for a clinical behavior therapy program and found that these seniors were easy to train, effective, and they got a good deal out of the experience themselves: "Doctor, *this* is medicine for *me*!" (Stumphauzer, Fantuzzo, Lane, & Sanchez, 1980). As funding becomes increasingly difficult for social programs, mobilizing and training volunteers and seniors is one path to explore. It might prove to be more effective and an enriching experience for each community in the long run.

As you have seen in Chapter Nine, schools play a vital role in the delinquent behavior equation. Schools are such a usual fixture in the community that we take the buildings themselves for granted. It is full of youngsters in the daytime and is perhaps used for some adult classes in the evening. Otherwise, schools are a largely unused community resource with a good deal of potential for community programs. Three school based programs will be noted here: one an unconventional use of schools and two prevention programs.

John Burchard (a pioneer in helping delinquents change) and some of his colleagues took such a step when they developed a voluntary, drop-in youth center in one school in Vermont (Stahl, Fuller, Lefebvre, & Burchard, 1979). The program was carried out in three phases:

1. a behavioral analysis of the youth center,
2. focus on youths having academic and social problems, and

3. shaping of behavior and gradual phasing in of adults and youths taking over operation of the program.

Impact on this community, through this development of an existing neighborhood resource, was achieved. Behaviors of youths were improved while, at the same time, recreational and educational resources were made available for any youngster who wanted to drop in.

Hartman (1979) demonstrated that a coping and social skills program in high school could *prevent* future problems. The program taught anxiety management, stress inoculation and social skills training to students at four levels of "risk" with short-term effects which held up at three month follow-up. (See Chapter Seven for more details on social skills training and Chapter Ten for stress inoculation.) Similarly, another school program (PREP) evaluated the effectiveness of a four-element school prevention program: (a) individualized programming for math and English for those students who were both referred and volunteered to participate, (b) group interpersonal skills classes, (c) a behavioral educational and counseling program for parents, and (d) teacher/staff training (Filipczak, Friedman, & Reese, 1979). The preventative effects of this school-based package were demonstrated and remained in effect at one year follow-up.

Most juvenile courts send "hard core" delinquents (serious and repeat offenders) to closed institutions, and very little has been done directly in the community as an alternative. One remarkable social learning program has achieved this goal. Davidson and Robinson (1975) developed a comprehensive behavioral community program for virtually *all* youths coming through the juvenile court. The program is noteworthy because it was truly comprehensive and involved the following elements:

1. keeping youths in their own home,
2. youths picked up at home by bus every day,
3. public works each morning for wages,
4. afternoon school based on programmed instruction,
5. behavioral group sessions twice a week, and
6. an overall level and point system.

The only obvious extension of social learning programs for

changing delinquent behavior that was not included was work with the family—behavioral family contracting (Chapter Six).

Community-based programs have developed in England as well. Reid, Feldman, and Ostapiuk (1980) report a three phase program called, aptly enough, SHAPE. In that program, offenders age 16 to 23 are placed (in phase I) in a group home with a relatively high level of control, reinforcement, and shaping of social skills. In Phase II these youths move into two-person housing with continued shaping of social and employment skills, but with increased self-management. Finally (in Phase III), independent living and employment are shaped. In visiting this program, the author was especially struck by SHAPE's application in a very "tough" part of Birmingham, England, and by the utilization of inexpensive, "short-life" housing (i.e., property not currently used and set for demolition at a later date).

An entirely different approach to modifying delinquent behavior is to attempt to study and understand it where it is happening and, then, to intervene directly on a community wide basis to change or, even better, prevent the behavior. We have tried to do just that in a youth gang-dominated community program we called "East Side Story" (Stumphauzer, Aiken, & Veloz, 1977).

We began with a multilevel behavioral analysis of one neighborhood: the youth gang, parents, police "gang unit" that patrolled the area, and the physical attributes of this same community. This was carried out "on the spot" through direct observation, video recording, and behavioral analysis interviews. Results suggested a multidetermined social learning of gang violence: a powerful behavior, modeled and reinforced by many sources. Little in the way of effective punishment was found. For example, the process of arrest/short-term detention/release appeared to act as *positive* reinforcement and not as punishment! A preliminary model of "learning gang violence" is found in Figure 7.

In some ways the most fascinating results of these years of study was a new focus on the nondelinquent (already discussed in Chapter Two). We completed a comprehensive behavioral analysis of two nondelinquent brothers who lived in that same gang-dominated community, and found that nondelinquent, productive behavior was being learned "with all the odds stacked against it" (Aiken, Stumphauzer, & Veloz, 1977). Aiken (1981) went on to study a group of nondelinquents in this community with the use of "beepers" or paging devices which signaled these youngsters to

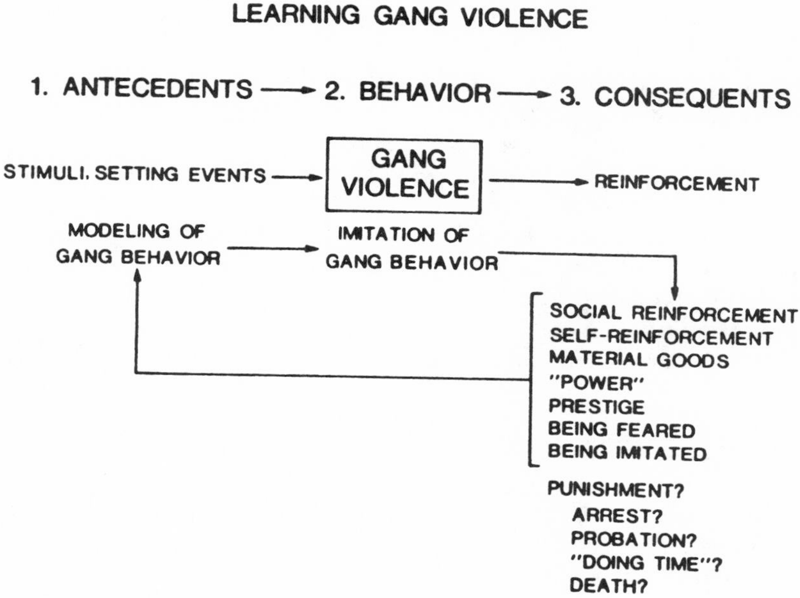

LEARNING GANG VIOLENCE

1. ANTECEDENTS ⟶ 2. BEHAVIOR ⟶ 3. CONSEQUENTS

FIGURE 7. Learning gang violence.

record their behavior and immediate environment at the moment. Potential implications for prevention were many, and are discussed below.

These behavioral analyses of the "big picture" of gang violence and nondelinquent behavior in this community led, in part, to a series of behavioral community anticrime programs (Stumphauzer, 1982). The author acted as consultant and evaluator for these programs and encouraged and taught the use of social learning principles to the community-based paraprofessionals who developed and ran the programs on the streets.

For example, three of the programs engaged previously hard-core gang members in behavior that was incompatible with delinquent gang behavior: (a) a "dial-an-escort" service, in which gang members would accompany senior citizens and women to cash their checks and do shopping so that they would *not* be robbed; (b) a community revitalization program in which youths canvased their own neighborhood block by block to evaluate "high crime" properties (e.g., vacant houses), and learned legal means to correct the problems; and (c) a street-theater group in which teenagers wrote, directed, and produced anticrime plays and skits (e.g., on gang violence and drug abuse) and presented them to peers and other community groups.

All six of the programs encouraged and reinforced behavior incompatible with crime and actively removed or limited some of the many reinforcers for gang delinquency listed in Figure 4 (attention, praise, freedom from prosecution, material goods) by organizing and educating parents' groups. One group of mothers even intervened directly in gang violence and would not only remove reinforcement from a gang member, but also not hesitate to walk up and take the gun out of his hand!

HOW TO DO BEHAVIORAL ANALYSES OF COMMUNITIES

How does one do a behavioral analysis of a community-wide problem? How does it differ from doing a behavioral analysis of one delinquent? As noted in Chapter Three, Kanfer and Saslow (1969) have developed a conceptual framework that is very useful in organizing information and in understanding one person—even a juvenile delinquent. Compare it with the following. My colleagues and I have expanded Kanfer and Saslow's seven point schema for behavioral analyses into a seven part conceptual framework for looking at community-wide problems (Stumphauzer, Veloz, & Aiken, 1981). It was used in the "East Side Story" analysis just described. More specifically, behavioral analyses of communities includes the following.

1. Initial Analysis of the Community

(a) What are the good attributes of the community (physical, social, economic), the community assets? (b) What are the major community problems or excesses? (c) What is lacking, what are the community deficits?

2. Clarification of Community Situation

(a) Who objects to the problem behaviors and who supports them? (b) Who objects to the asset behaviors and who supports them? (c) Under exactly what circumstances do they occur?

3. Motivational Analysis

(a) How does this community utilize incentives (reinforcers and punishments)? (b) Who has control of incentives? (c) What incentives for behavior change are potentially available?

4. Developmental Analysis

(a) How did this community develop economically, ethnically, and politically? (b) What are the physical assets and limitations of this community?

5. Analysis of Self-Control

(a) How does this community control its own problems? (b) What circumstances increase or decrease community self-control?

6. Analysis of Social Relationships

(a) Who are the most influencial and significant people in this community? (b) Exactly how do they exercise their influence on the behavior of residents?

7. Analysis of Socio-Cultural-Physical Environment

(a) What are the norms in this community for these behaviors? (b) What community support and resistance is there for changing behavior problems? (c) What community interventions follow logically from this analysis?

Finally, how can all of this objective, behavioral analysis information be synthesized to form conclusions about how a particular neighborhood or community is teaching, learning and maintaining both delinquent and nondelinquent behavior? These conclusions then form the basis for community intevention or prevention programs. This is the parallel for an individual "treatment plan." This approach has direct utility and applicability and is, therefore, a considerable advance from simply labeling ("a high crime neighborhood") and theorizing ("caused by poverty") about community problems. This model needs to be further evaluated in other communities.

PREVENTION OF DELINQUENT BEHAVIOR

"Rehabilitating delinquents is not necessarily the best way of reducing the problem of delinquency. In terms of human values, personal happiness and money, prevention represents a higher goal than rehabilitation" (Sarason, 1978, p. 312). While this author shares this view with Sarason, not everyone does. For example, two psychiatrists have argued against putting major effort into primary prevention (Lamb & Zusman, 1979). They suggest that "real" or "genuine mental illness" cannot be prevented.

Albee (1982) disagreed with their view and argued that prevention is not only possible, but the most humanistic of goals. In Chapter One, the author discussed the futility of the mental illness model of delinquency and promoted the view of learned delinquent behavior. If one truly accepts the view that delinquent behavior is learned and can be unlearned (the central thesis of this book), then it also follows that delinquent behavior can be prevented. Is this the ultimate answer to the problem of delinquency?

The National Crime Prevention Institute (1978) suggested the following equation: ability + opportunity + desire = crime. Elsewhere (Stumphauzer, 1981b) the author redefined this formula in more social learning terms:

CRIME REPERTOIRE + STIMULI AND SETTING EVENTS + PERCEIVED REINFORCEMENT = CRIMINAL BEHAVIOR

Crime prevention programs must remove some (or a combination) of these elements from the formula. Several such crime-prevention strategies are possible and lend themselves particularly well to a social learning approach.

One such strategy, already explored above in the "East Side Story" program, is the study of youths in high-crime neighborhoods who do *not* become delinquent. If we completely understood how these youths *learn to stay out of trouble,* despite the odds against them and without intervention from any professional agencies, we might be able to teach this naturally occurring self-control (a) directly to younger children or (b) indirectly to parents in the form of childrearing for nondelinquency. Such naturally effective youths could become especially strong peer-models. Surely this could be more successful than the usual trial-and-too-often-error method of growing up in tough neighborhoods.

A related, second strategy could be to *develop behavior that is incompatible with crime* (noncrime repertoire). It could include such obvious behaviors as (a) attending school, (b) working, (c) being active in sports, (d) participating in social and recreational clubs, and (e) increased contact with noncriminal models (peers & family). It may sound as if the best way to keep young people out of trouble (especially in an environment in which crime is highly probable) is to fill their day (and night) with *other* activities. Exactly. Davidson and Robinson (1975) practically did just that with the comprehensive community program described earlier in this chapter. Although those youths undoubtedly still had the ability to do crimes, the boys were kept busy in a comprehensive program, and reinforcement was switched to behaviors incompatible with delinquent behavior and setting events (people and places) were changed.

A third approach is to change the environment itself to prevent crime—to directly change the opportunity or stimuli/setting events. In a very refreshing book, Jeffery (1977) discussed just how to *prevent crime through environmental design.* Urban planning and design possibilities are far-reaching and are quite compatible with a social learning approach to delinquent behavior. This might include everything from simply adding street lights to the comprehensive redesign of inner cities. For example, *before a crime is committed,* it might be prevented through the following types of environmental/behavioral engineering: surveillance systems, urban planning and design, removal of the opportunities to commit criminal acts, citizen education, and the rewarding of lawful behavior. Clarke (1980) has discussed similar theory and crime prevention practices in Great Britain and Europe.

Finally, is total crime prevention possible? It might be possible, but it seems highly unlikely for several reasons. Reformulating the question sheds some light on the issues: Is delinquency prevention reinforcing? It would appear not. At this time there is relatively little interest or funding available for delinquency prevention programs. Indeed, there is probably less money available today than there was ten years ago. The bulk of governmental anticrime budgets goes for continuation of justice, corrections, and treatment programs. Delinquency prevention would put thousands out of work. Many find their current behaviors of arresting, defending, prosecuting, judging, correcting, and therapizing highly reinforcing—even when there is no behavior change! Institutions and people are slow to change, and currently most of the reinforcers are stacked toward maintaining the current, largely ineffective system.

What does the future hold? Elsewhere (in a suggested reading, Stumphauzer, 1981a), the author has outlined possible and probable future developments in seven areas: (a) juvenile court, (b) institutions, (c) probation, (d) group homes, (e) clinical behavior therapy, (f) community-based programs, and (g) prevention.

One final point is that the prevention of delinquent behavior takes a long time and is difficult to prove. For this and other reasons, governments appear to be more interested in such short-term goals as crime detection and prosecution rather than the longer range prevention of delinquent behavior. Although crime prevention may well be more cost-effective in the long run, politicians and policy makers appear unwilling to support expensive programs whose results may be several years in coming. When those years do arrive, will we still be doing the same cost-ineffective things? What would it take to change *our* behavior so that we could help delinquents change?

SUMMARY

Delinquent behavior, for the most part, occurs in the community: in city streets, parks, in stores, in cars. Most of the antecedents and consequents that control delinquent behavior (the ABCs of Chapter One) are in the neighborhood or community as well. This chapter reviewed social learning programs that have tried to understand, prevent, or change delinquent behavior in its natural habitat—in the community. While showing great promise as an "ultimate answer" to the problem of delinquency, this approach runs counter to traditional programs of having each youth go to a place to be "corrected" or "treated." Short-sighted politicians and professionals act to maintain current programs of institutionalization, the "mental health industry," and the "get tough" programs of juvenile justice. At the same time, budgets have been cut for broader community programs which might have had long-term gains.

Several innovative community approaches were reviewed. In one, delinquents were "recruited" on street corners and were worked with in a local storefront. In another, behavioral consultation was given to a tenants association group in a high crime housing project. Three school-based prevention programs were reviewed. Other programs utilized volunteers, developed comprehensive activities, and utilized a three phase system to shape nondelinquent behavior. A seven point scheme for behavioral analyses of communities was outlined. The author and colleagues conducted two parallel behavioral analyses in one high juvenile crime community: one of the violent youth gang that dominated that neighborhood and another of nondelinquent youth in the same setting. These behavioral analyses led, in part, to a series of community anticrime programs.

Social learning perspectives on the prevention of delinquent behavior were presented. Three possible approaches were discussed. One was the study of youths in any given community who do *not* become delinquent in the hope of expanding this naturally occurring prevention. A related, second strategy was to develop behaviors in a community that are *incompatible* with crime. A third approach was to physically change a community (or to design for crime prevention through city planning). Finally, total delinquency prevention was seen as possible but unlikely to occur. Years hence, will we be as ineffective at helping delinquents change as we are today? What would it take to change *our* behavior so that we could help delinquents change?

READINGS

1. Feldman, P. (1983). Juvenile offending: Behavioral approaches to prevention and intervention. *Child and Family Behavior Therapy, 5,* 37–50.

2. Jeffery, C. R. (1977). *Crime prevention through environmental design.* Beverly Hills: Sage.

3. Stumphauzer, J. S. (1981a). Behavioral approaches to juvenile delinquency: Future perspectives. In L. Michelson, M. Hersen, & S. M. Turner (Eds. *Future perspectives in behavior therapy.* New York: Plenum Press, 65–80.

References

Aiken, T. W. (1981). *Behavior analysis of nondelinquent invulnerable adolescents from a high juvenile crime community by way of experiential sampling*. Unpublished doctoral dissertation, University of Southern California, Los Angeles.

Aiken, T. W., Stumphauzer, J. S., & Veloz, E. V. (1977). Behavioral analysis of nondelinquent brothers in a high juvenile crime community. *Behavioral Disorders, 2,* 212–222.

Albee, G. W. (1982). Preventing psychopathology and promoting human potential. *American Psychologist, 37,* 1043–1050.

Alexander, J. F., & Parsons, B. V. (1973). Short-term behavioral intervention with delinquent families: Impact on family process and recidivism. *Journal of Abnormal Psychology, 81,* 219–225.

Allen, J. D., Phillips, E. L., Phillips, E., Fixsen, D. L., & Wolf, M. M. (1972). *Achievement place: A novel*. Unpublished manuscript, University of Kansas.

Allison, T. S., Kendall, S., & Sloane, D. (1979). New directions in a juvenile hall setting. In J. S. Stumphauzer (Ed.), *Progress in behavior therapy with delinquents*. Springfield, IL: Thomas.

American Psychiatric Association (1980). *Diagnostic and statistical manual of mental disorders* (third edition). Washington, D.C.

Argyle, M. (1969). *Social interaction*. London: Methuen.

Atkeson, B. M., & Forehand, R. (1982). Conduct disorders. In E. J. Mash & L. G. Terdal (Eds.), *Behavioral assessment of childhood disorders*. New York: Guilford.

Ayllon, T., & Azrin, N. H. (1968). *The token economy*. New York: Appleton-Century-Crofts.

Azrin, N. H., Flores, T., & Kaplan, S. J. (1975). Job-finding club: A group-assisted program for obtaining employment. *Behavior Research and Therapy, 13,* 17–27.

Bailey, J. S., Wolf, M. M., & Phillips, E. L. (1970). Home-based reinforcement and the modification of pre-delinquent classroom behavior. *Journal of Applied Behavior Analysis, 3,* 223–233.

Bandura, A. (1969). *Principles of behavior modification*. New York: Holt, Rinehart, and Winston.

Bandura, A. (1977). *Social learning theory*. Englewood Cliffs, NJ: Prentice Hall.

Bandura, A., Ross, D., & Ross, A. (1963). Imitation of film-mediated aggressive models. *Journal of Abnormal and Social Psychology, 66,* 3–11.

Bedell, J. R., & Archer, R. P. (1980). Peer managed token economies: Evaluation and description. *Journal of Clinical Psychology, 36,* 716–722.

Braukmann, C. J., Maloney, D. M., Fixsen, D. L., Phillips, E. L., & Wolf, M. M. (1974). Analysis of a selection interview training package. *Criminal Justice and Behavior, 1,* 30–42.

Buehler, R. E., Patterson, G. R., Furniss, J. M. (1966). The reinforcement of behavior in institutional settings. *Behavior Research and Therapy, 4,* 157–167.

Burkhart, B. R., Behles, M. W., & Stumphauzer, J. S. (1976). Training juvenile probation officers in behavior modification: Knowledge, attitude change, or behavioral competence? *Behavior Therapy, 7,* 47–53.

Camp, B. W. (1976). Verbal mediation in young aggressive boys. *Journal of Abnormal Psychology, 86,* 145–153.

Camp, B. W., Blom, G. E. Hebert, F., & vanDoornick, W. J. (1977). "Think aloud": A program for developing self-control in young aggressive boys. *Journal of Abnormal Child Psychology, 5,* 157–169.

Carney, L. P. (1977). *Probation and parole: Legal and social dimensions.* New York: McGraw-Hill.

Cartledge, G., & Milburn, J. F. (Eds.) (1980). *Teaching social skills to children: Innovative approaches.* New York: Pergamon.

Cautela, J. R. (1967). Covert sensitization. *Psychological Reports, 20,* 459–468.

Clarke, R. G. V. (1980). Situational crime prevention—theory and practice. *The British Journal of Criminology, 20,* 136–147.

Clement, P. W. (1975). *Guidelines for observing your child's behavior.* Unpublished manuscript, Fuller Graduate School of Psychology, Pasadena, CA.

Cobb, J. A., & Ray, R. S. (1975). Manual for coding discrete behaviors in the school setting. In G. R. Patterson et al. (Eds.), *A social learning approach to family intervention.* Eugene, OR: Castalia.

Cohen, H. L., & Filipczak, J. (1971). *A new learning environment.* San Francisco: Jossey-Bass.

Cohen, H. L., Filipczak, J. A., Bis, J. S., & Cohen, J. E. (1966). *C.A.S.E.: Contingencies applicable to special education of delinquents.* Washington, D.C.: U.S. Department of Health Education and Welfare.

Craighead, W. E., Kazdin, A. E., & Mahoney, M. J. (1981). *Behavior modification: Principles, issues, and applications.* Boston: Houghton-Mifflin.

Davidson, W. S., & Robinson, M. J. (1975). Community psychology and behavior modification: A community based program for the prevention of delinquency. *Journal of Corrective Psychiatry and Behavior Therapy, 21,* 1–12.

DeRisi, W. J., & Butz, G. (1975). *Writing behavioral contracts: A case simulation practice manual.* Champaign, IL: Research Press.

Diebert, A. N., & Golden, F. (1973). Behavior modification workshop with juvenile officers: Brief report. *Behavior Therapy, 4,* 586–588.

Douds, A. F., Engelsgjerd, M., & Collingwood, T. R. (1977). Behavior contracting with youthful offenders and their parents. *Child Welfare, 56,* 409–417.

D'Zurilla, T. J., & Goldfried, M. R. (1971). Problem-solving and behavior modification. *Journal of Abnormal Psychology, 78,* 107–126.

Eysenck, H. J. (1964). *Crime and personality.* Boston: Houghton-Mifflin.

Falloon, I.R.H., Lindley, R., McDonald, R, & Marks, I. M. (1977). Social skills training of out-patient groups: A controlled study of rehearsal and homework. *British Journal of Psychiatry, 131,* 599–609.

Federal Bureau of Investigation. (1976). *Uniform Crime Reports.* Washington, D.C.: Department of Justice.

Feindler, E. L., & Fremouw, W. J. (1983). Stress inoculation training for adolescent anger problems. In D. Meichenbaum & M. E. Jaremko (Eds.) *Stress reduction and prevention.* New York: Plenum Press.

Feldman, P. (1983). Juvenile offending: Behavioral approaches to prevention and intervention. *Child and Family Behavior Therapy, 5,* 37–50.

Filipczak, J., Friedman, R. M., & Reese, S. C. (1979). PREP: Educational programming to prevent juvenile problems. In J. S. Stumphauzer (Ed.), *Progress in behavior therapy with delinquents.* Springfield, IL: Thomas.

Fiordaliso, R., Lordeman, A., Filipczak, J., & Friedman, R. M. (1976). *Decreasing absenteeism on the junior high school level.* Paper presented at the meeting of the American Educational Research Association, San Francisco.

Fischer, D. G. (1983). Parental supervision and delinquency. *Perceptual and Motor Skills, 56,* 635–640.

Fixsen, D. L., Phillips, E. L., & Wolf, M. M. (1973). Achievement place: Experiments in self-government with predelinquents. *Journal of Applied Behavior Analysis, 6,* 31–47.

Fleischman, M. J., Conger, R. E. (1977). *The T.E.A.C.H. manual: Specific techniques for management of aggressive children.* Unpublished manuscript, Oregon Social Learning Center.

Fleisher, B. M. (1966). *The economics of delinquency.* Chicago: Quadrangle Books.

Fo, W. S. O., & O'Donnell, C. R. (1974). The buddy system: Relationship and contingency conditions in a community intervention program for youth with nonprofessionals as behavior change agents. *Journal of Consulting and Clinical Psychology, 42,* 163–169.

Forehand, R. L., & McMahon, R. J. (1981). *Helping the noncompliant child: A clinician's guide to parent training.* New York: Guilford.

Freedman, B. J., Rosenthal, L., Donahoe, C. P., Schlundt, D. G., & McFall, R. M. (1978). A social-behavioral analysis of skill deficits in delinquent and nondelinquent adolescent boys. *Journal of Consulting and Clinical Psychology, 46,* 1448–1462.

Gaffney, L. R., & McFall, R. M. (1981). A comparison of social skills in delinquent and nondelinquent adolescent girls using a behavioral role-playing inventory. *Journal of Consulting and Clinical Psychology, 49,* 959–967.

Gibbons, D. C. (1970). *Delinquent Behavior.* Englewood Cliffs, NJ: Prentice-Hall.

Glenwick, D., & Jason, L. (Eds.). (1980). *Behavioral community psychology: Progress and prospects.* New York: Praeger.

Goldfried, M. R., & Davison, G. C. (1976). *Clinical behavior therapy.* New York: Holt, Rinehart and Winston.

Goldstein, A. P., Sprafkin, R. P., Gershaw, N. J., & Klein, P. (1980). *Skill-streaming the adolescent.* Champaign, IL: Research Press.

Goocher, B. E. (1984). Some additional perspectives on current trends: A comment on LeCroy. *Child Care Quarterly, 13,* 98–101.

Greenberger, E., & Steinberg, L. D. (1981). *Part-time employment of in school youth: An assessment of costs and benefits.* Unpublished manuscript, University of California, Irvine.

Gross, A. M., Brigham, T. A., Hopper, C., & Bologna, N. C. (1980). Self-management and social skills training. *Criminal Justice and Behavior, 7,* 161–184.

Hartman, L. M. (1979). The preventative reduction of psychological risk in asymptomatic adolescents. *American Journal of Orthopsychiatry, 49,* 121–135.

Heward, W. L., McCormick, S. H., & Joynes, Y. (1980). Completing job applications: Evaluation of an instructional program for mildly retarded delinquents. *Behavioral Disorders, 5,* 223–234.

Hindelang, M. J., Hirschi, T., & Weis, J. G. (1981). *Measuring delinquency.* Beverly Hills: Sage.

Jeffery, C. R. (1977). *Crime prevention through environmental design.* Beverly Hills: Sage.

Jesness, C. F. (1975). Comparative effectiveness of behavior modification and transactional analysis programs for delinquents. *Journal of Consulting and Clinical Psychology, 43,* 758–779.

Jesness, C. F. (1976). The youth center project: Transactional analysis and behavior modification programs for dellinquents. *Behavioral Disorders, 1,* 27–36.

Jesness, C. F., & DeRisi, W. (1973). Some variations in techniques of contingency management in a school for delinquents. In J. S. Stumphauzer (Ed.), *Behavior therapy with delinquents.* Springfield, IL: Thomas.

Johnson, A. M., & Szurek, S. A. (1952). The genesis of antisocial acting out in children and adults. *Psychoanalytic Quarterly, 21,* 323–343.

Johnson, S. M., Christensen, A., & Bellamy, G. T. (1976). Evaluation of family intervention through unobtrusive audio recordings. *Journal of Applied Behavior Analysis, 9,* 213–219.

Kanfer, F. H. (1977). *Helping people change.* New York: Pergamon Press.

Kanfer, F. H., & Karoly, P. (1972). Self-control: A behavioristic excursion into the lion's den. *Behavior Therapy, 3,* 398–416.

Kanfer, F. H., & Saslow, G. (1969). Behavior diagnosis. In C. M. Franks (Ed.), *Behavior therapy: Appraisal and status.* New York: McGraw Hill.

Karacki, L., & Levinson, R. B. (1970). A token economy in a correctional institution for youthful offenders. *The Howard Journal of Penology and Crime Prevention, 13*, 20–30.

Kazdin, A. E. (1977) *The token economy.* New York: Plenum.

Kirigin, K. A., Braukmann, C. J., Atwater, J. D., & Wolf, M. M. (1982). An evaluation of teaching family (Achievement Place) group homes for juvenile offenders. *Journal of Applied Behavior Analysis, 15*, 1–16.

Kirigin, K. A., Wolf, M. M., Braukmann, C. J., Fixsen, D. L., & Phillips, E. L. (1979). Achievement Place: A preliminary outcome evaluation. In J. S. Stumphauzer (Ed.), *Progress in behavior therapy with delinquents.* Springfield, IL: Thomas.

Lamb, H. R., & Zusman, J. (1979). Primary prevention in perspective. *American Journal of Psychiatry, 136*, 12–17.

LeCroy, C. W. (Ed.) (1983). *Social skills training for children and youth.* New York: Haworth Press.

LeCroy, C. W. (1984). Residential treatment services: A review of some current trends. *Child Care Quarterly, 13*, 83–97.

Liberman, R. P., Ferris, C., Salgado, P., & Salgado, J. (1975). Replication of the Achievement Place model in California. *Journal of Applied Behavior Analysis, 8*, 287–299.

Little, V. L., & Kendall, P. C. (1979). Cognitive-behavioral interventions with delinquents: Problem solving, role-taking, and self-control. In P. C. Kendall & S. D. Hollon (Eds.), *Cognitive-behavioral interventions: Theory, research, and procedures.* New York: Academic Press.

MacCulloch, M. J., Williams, C., & Birtles, C. J. (1971). The successful application of aversion therapy to an adolescent exhibitionist. *Journal of Behavior Therapy and Experimental Psychiatry, 2*, 61–66.

Mahoney, M. J. (1974). *Cognition and behavior modification.* Cambridge, MA: Ballinger.

Mahoney, M. J. (1977). Reflections on the cognitive-learning trend in psychotherapy. *American Psychologist, 32*, 5–13.

Mahoney, M. J. (1979). Cognitive issues in the treatment of delinquency. In J. S. Stumphauzer (Ed.), *Progress in behavior therapy with delinquents.* Springfield, IL: Thomas.

Mash, E. J., & Terdal, L. G. (Eds.) (1981). *Behavioral assessment of childhood disorders.* New York: Guilford.

Massimo, J. L., & Shore, M. F. (1963). A comprehensive vocationally oriented psychotherapeutic program for delinquent boys. *The American Journal of Orthopsychiatry, 33*, 634–642.

Mayer, G. R., Butterworth, T., Nafpaktitis, M., & Sulzer-Azaroff, B. (1983). Preventing school vandalism and improving discipline: A three year study. *Journal of Applied Behavior Analysis, 16*, 355–369.

McCord, W., & McCord, J. (1964). *The psychopath: An essay on the criminal mind.* Princeton, NJ: Van Nostrand.

McCullough, J. P., Huntsinger, G. M., & Nay, W. R. (1977). Self-control treatment of aggression in a 16-year-old male. *Journal of Consulting and Clinical Psychology, 45*, 322–331.

Meichenbaum, D. M. (1977). *Cognitive behavior modification.* New York: Plenum.

Meichenbaum, D. M., Bowers, K. S., & Ross, R. R. (1968). Modification of classroom behavior of institutionalized female adolescent offenders. *Behavior Research and Therapy, 6*, 343–353.

Michelson, L., Wood, R., & Flynn, J. (1982). *Long-term follow-up of an Achievement Place residential treatment center for delinquent youths.* Unpublished manuscript, University of Pittsburgh.

Mills, C. M., & Walter, T. L. (1979). Reducing juvenile delinquency: A behavioral-employment intervention program. In J. S. Stumphauzer (Ed.), *Progress in behavior therapy with delinquents.* Springfield, IL: Thomas.

National Crime Prevention Institute (1978). *Crime prevention.* Washington, D.C.: U.S. Department of Justice.

Nietzel, M. T. (1979). *Crime and its modification: A social learning perspective.* New York: Pergamon.

Nietzel, M. T., Winett, R. A., MacDonald, M. L., & Davidson, W. S. (1977). *Behavioral approaches to community psychology.* New York: Pergamon.

Novaco, R. (1975). *Anger control: The development and evaluation of an experimental treatment.* Lexington, MA: Heath.

Nye, F. I., & Short, J. F. (1957). Scaling delinquent behavior. *American Sociological Review, 22,* 326–331.

O'Leary, K. D., & O'Leary, S. G. (1972). *Classroom management: The successful use of behavior modification.* New York: Pergamon Press.

Ollendick, T. H., & Hersen, M. (1979). Social skills training for delinquents. *Behavior Research and Therapy, 17,* 547–554.

Ollendick, T. H., & Hersen, M. (Eds.) (1984). *Child behavioral assessment: Principles and procedures.* New York: Pergamon Press.

Patterson, G. R. (1982). *Coercive family process.* Eugene, OR: Castalia.

Patterson, G. R., Reid, J. B., Jones, R. R., & Conger, R. E. (1975). *A social learning approach to family intervention.* Eugene, OR: Castalia.

Phillips, E. L. (1968). Achievement Place: Token reinforcement procedures in a home-style rehabilitation setting for "predelinquent" boys. *Journal of Applied Behavior Analysis, 1,* 213–223.

Phillips, E. L., Phillips, E. A., Fixsen, D. L., & Wolf, M. M. (1974). *The teaching-family handbook.* Lawrence, KS: University of Kansas Printing Service.

Pines, M. (1979). Superkids. *Psychology Today, 12,* 53–63.

Polakow, R. L., & Doctor, R. M. (1973). Treatment of marijuana and barbiturate dependency by contingency contracting. *Journal of Behavior Therapy and Experimental Psychiatry, 4,* 375–377.

Polakow, R. L., & Doctor, R. M. (1974a). *Establishing behavior therapy in a public agency.* Paper presented at the Association for Advancement of Behavior Therapy, Chicago.

Polakow, R. L., & Doctor, R. M. (1974b). A behavior modification program for adult drug offenders. *Journal of Research in Crime and Delinquency, 3,* 41–45.

Polakow, R. L., & Peabody, D. L. (1975). Behavioral treatment of child abuse. *International Journal of Offender Therapy and Comparative Criminology, 19,* 100–103.

Powers, M. D. (1984). Syndromal diagnosis and the behavioral assessment of childhood disorders. *Child and Family Behavior Therapy, 6,* 1–15.

Quay, H. C., & Peterson, D. R. (1974). *Manual for the behavior problem checklist.* Unpublished manuscript, University of Miami.

Rathus, S. A. (1973). A 30-item schedule for assessing assertive behavior. *Behavior Therapy, 4,* 398–406.

Reckless, W. C., Dinitz, S., & Murray, E. (1957). The good boy in a high delinquency area. *Journal of Criminal Law, Criminology, and Police Science, 48,* 18–25.

Reid, I. D. (1982). A behavioral regime in a secure youth treatment center. In M. P. Feldman (Ed.), *Developments in the study of criminal behavior. Volume 1: The prevention and control of offending.* London: Wiley.

Reid, I. D., Feldman, M. P., & Ostapiuk, E. (1980). The shape project for young offenders: Introduction and overview. *Journal of Offender Counseling, Services & Rehabilitation, 4,* 233–246.

Risley, T. (1972). *Juniper gardens.* Presented at the American Psychological Association convention, Honolulu.

Robin, A. L., & Foster, S. L. (in press). *Parent-adolescent problem solving and communication.* New York: Guilford.

Sarason, I. G. (1978). A cognitive social learning approach to juvenile delinquency. In R. D.

Hare & D. Schalling (Eds.), *Psychopathic behavior: Approaches to research*. New York: Wiley.

Scarpitti, F. R., Murray, E., Dinitz, S., & Reckless, W. C. (1960). The "good" boy in a high delinquency area: four years later. *American Sociological Review, 25*, 555–558.

Schloss, P. J., Kane, M. S., & Miller, S. (1981). Truancy intervention with behavior disordered adolescents. *Behavioral Disorders, 6*, 175–179.

Schwitzgebel, R. (1964). *Street corner research: An experimental approach to the juvenile delinquent*. Cambridge, MA: Harvard University Press.

Shoemaker, M. E. (1979). Group assertion training for institutionalized male delinquents. In J. S. Stumphauzer (Ed.), *Progress in behavior therapy with delinquents*. Springfield, IL: Thomas.

Shore, M. F., & Massimo, J. L. (1979). Fifteen years after treatment: A follow-up study of comprehensive vocationally-oriented psychotherapy. *American Journal of Orthopsychiatry, 49*, 240–245.

Skinner, B. F. (1953). *Science and human behavior*. New York: MacMillan.

Smith, R. R., Milan, M. A., Wood, L. F., & McKee, J. M. (1976). The correctional officer as a behavioral technician. *Criminal Justice and Behavior, 3*, 345–360.

Spence, A. J., & Spence, S. H. (1980). Cognitive changes associated with social skills training. *Behavior Research and Therapy, 18*, 265–272.

Spence, S. (1979). Social skills training with adolescent offenders: A review. *Behavioral Psychotherapy, 7*, 49–56.

Spence, S. (1980). *Social skills training with children and adolescents*. London: NFER Publishing.

Spence, S. H. (1981). Validation of social skills of adolescent males in an interview conversation with a previously unknown adult. *Journal of Applied Behavior Analysis, 14*, 159–168.

Spence, S. H., & Marzillier, J. S. (1979). Social skills training with adolescent, male offenders: Short term effects. *Behavior Research and Therapy, 17*, 7–16.

Spivack, G., Platt, J. J., & Shure, M. B. (1976). *The problem solving approach to adjustment*. San Francisco: Jossey-Bass.

Stahl, J. R., Fuller, E. J., Lefebvre, M. F., & Burchard, J. (1979). The token-economy youth center: A model for programming peer reinforcement. In J. S. Stumphauzer (Ed.), *Progress in behavior therapy with delinquents*. Springfield, IL: Thomas.

Steinberg, L., Greenberger, E., Jacobi, M., & Garduque, L. (1981). Working: A partial antidote to adolescent egocentrism. *Journal of Youth and Adolescence, 10*, 141–157.

Stephens, T. M. (1981). Teaching social behavior—the schools' challenge in the 1980's. *The Directive Teacher, 3*, 4–10.

Stuart, R. B. (1970). Assessment and change of the communicational patterns of juvenile delinquents and their parents. In R. D. Rubin (Ed.), *Advances in Behavior Therapy*. New York: Academic Press.

Stuart, R. B. (1971). Behavioral contracting within the families of delinquents. *Journal of Behavior Therapy and Experimental Psychiatry, 2*, 1–11.

Stuart, R. B., & Lott, L. A. (1972). Behavioral contracting with delinquents: A cautionary note. *Journal of Behavior Therapy and Experimental Psychiatry, 3*, 161–169.

Stumphauzer, J. S. (1972). Increased delay of gratification in young prison inmates through exposure to high-delay peer-models. *Journal of Personality and Social Psychology, 21*, 10–17.

Stumphauzer, J. S. (Ed.) (1973). *Behavior therapy with delinquents*. Springfield, IL: Thomas.

Stumphauzer, J. S. (1974a). *Six techniques of modifying delinquent behavior*. Leona, NJ: Behavioral Sciences Tape Library.

Stumphauzer, J. S. (1974b) *Daily behavior card manual*. Box 1168, Venice, CA, 90291: Behaviormetrics.

Stumphauzer, J. S. (1976a). Modifying delinquent behavior: Beginnings and current practices. *Adolescence, 11,* 13–28.

Stumphauzer, J. S. (1976b). Elimination of stealing by self-reinforcement of alternative behavior and family contracting. *Journal of Behavior Therapy and Experimental Psychiatry, 7,* 265–268.

Stumphauzer, J. S. (1977). *Behavior modification principles: An introduction and training manual.* Box 1168, Venice, CA, 90291: Behaviormetrics.

Stumphauzer, J. S. (Ed.) (1979). *Progress in behavior therapy with delinquents.* Springfield, IL: Thomas.

Stumphauzer, J. S. (1980a). Learning to drink: Adolescents and alcohol. *Addictive Behavior, 5,* 277–283.

Stumphauzer, J. S. (1980b). A behavior analysis questionnaire for adolescent drinkers. *Psychological Reports, 47,* 641–642.

Stumphauzer, J. S. (1980c). Four community anticrime programs in East Los Angeles. *National Council of La Raza Reportero,* Issue 4, 2.

Stumphauzer, J. S. (1981a). Behavioral approaches to juvenile delinquency: Future perspectives. In L. Michelson, M. Hersen, & S. M. Turner (Eds.), *Future perspectives in behavior therapy.* New York: Plenum.

Stumphauzer, J. S. (1981b). Behavior modification with delinquents and criminals. In E. Craighead, A. Kazdin, & M. J. Mahoney (Eds.), *Behavior modification: Principles, issues, and applications* (second edition). Boston: Houghton-Mifflin.

Stumphauzer, J. S. (1983). Learning not to drink: Adolescents and abstinence. *Journal of Drug Education, 13,* 39–48.

Stumphauzer, J. S., Aiken, T. W., & Veloz, E. V. (1977). East side story: Behavioral analysis of a high juvenile crime community. *Behavioral Disorders, 2,* 76–84.

Stumphauzer, J. S., Candelora, K., & Venema, H. B. (1975). *Training probation investigators in behavioral analysis.* Unpublished manuscript: University of Southern California School of Medicine.

Stumphauzer, J. S., Candelora, K., & Venema, H. B. (1976). A follow-up of probation officers trained in behavior modification. *Behavior Therapy, 7,* 713–715.

Stumphauzer, J. S., & Davis, L. C. (1983a). Training community-based, Asian American mental health personnel in behavior modification. *Journal of Community Psychology, 11,* 253–258.

Stumphauzer, J. S., & Davis, L. C. (1983b). Training Mexican-American mental health personnel in behavior therapy. *Journal of Behavior Therapy and Experimental Psychiatry, 14,* 215–217.

Stumphauzer, J. S., Fantuzzo, J. W., Lane, P. J., & Sanchez, V. C. (1980). Training volunteer foster grandparents as behavior raters. *Child Behavior Therapy, 2,* 75–78.

Stumphauzer, J. S., & Perez, P. (1981). Learning to drink II: Peer survey of normal adolescents. *International Journal of the Addictions, 8,* 1363–1372.

Stumphauzer, J. S., Veloz, E. V., & Aiken, T. W. (1981). Behavioral analyses of communities: A challenge. *Psychological Reports, 49,* 343–346.

Teicher, J. D., Sinay, R. D., & Stumphauzer, J. S. (1976). Training community-based paraprofessionals as behavior therapists with families of alcohol abusing adolescents. *American Journal of Psychiatry, 7,* 265–268.

Tharp, R. G., & Wetzel, R. J. (1969). *Behavior modification in the natural environment.* New York: Academic Press.

Thoresen, C. E., & Mahoney, M. J. (1974). *Behavioral self-control.* New York: Holt.

Thoresen, K. E., Thoresen, C. E., Klein, S. B., Wilbur, C. S., Becker-Haven, J. F., & Haven, W. G. (1979). Learning House: Helping troubled children and their parents change themselves. In J. S. Stumphauzer (Ed.), *Progress in behavior therapy with delinquents,* Springfield, IL: Thomas.

Thorne, G. L., Tharp, R. G., & Wetzel, R. J. (1967). Behavior modification techniques: New tools for probation officers. *Federal Probation,* June, 21–27.

Tunley, R. (1964). *Crime and chaos: A world report on juvenile delinquency.* New York: Dell.

Tyler, V. O. (1967). Application of operant token reinforcement to the academic performance of an institutionalized delinquent. *Psychological Reports, 21,* 249–260.

Tyler, V. O., & Brown, G. D. (1967). The use of swift, brief isolation as a group control device for institutionalized delinquents. *Behavior Research and Therapy, 5,* 1–9.

Van Hasselt, V. B., Hersen, M., Whitehill, M. B., & Bellack, A. S. (1979). Social skill assessment and training for children: An evaluative review. *Behavior Research and Therapy, 17,* 413–437.

Walker, J. E., & Shea, T. M. (1980). *Behavior modification: A practical approach for educators.* St. Louis: Mosby.

West, D. J., & Farrington, D. P. (1973). *Who becomes delinquent?* London: Heinemann Educational.

Wood, G., Green, L., & Bry, B. H. (1982). The impact of behavioral training upon the knowledge and effectiveness of juvenile probation officers and volunteers. *Journal of Community Psychology, 10,* 133–141.

Wood, R., & Flynn, J. M. (1978) A self-evaluation token system versus an external evaluation token system alone in a residential setting with predelinquent youth. *Journal of Applied Behavior Analysis, 11,* 503–512.

Yates, B. T., Haven, W. G., & Thoresen, C. E. (1979). Cost-effectiveness anlysis at Learning House: How much change for how much money In J. S. Stumphauzer (Ed.), *Progress in behavior therapy with delinquents.* Springfield, IL: Thomas.

Yochelson, S., & Samenow, S. E. (1976). *The criminal personality.* New York: Jason Aronson.

Subject Index

Name Index

Williams, C. 151,200
Winett, R. A. 183,201
Wolf, M. M. 139,172,173,174,
    176,182,197,198,200,201
Wood, G. 128,136,204
Wood, L. F. 88,202
Wood, R. 84,174,200,204

Y

Yates, B. 175,204
Yochelson, S. 3,204

Z

Zusman, J. 192,200